The Coming of the King

in Matthew 24 and 25

Other Books by the Author

The Coming End of the Age

Preparing for the Lord's Return

The Goal and Peak of Our Christian Experience
Insights into Revelation, Book 1

The Beast, His Image, and His Mark
Insights into Revelation, Book 2

Firstfruits and Harvest
Insights into Revelation, Book 3

A Place Prepared
Insights into Revelation, Book 4

Delusion and God's Salvation

Greapa

Booklets by the Author

The Heart of God

The Heart of God II

The Heart of God III

The Heart of God IV

Redemption and Salvation

Signs of the End

Visit **aplaceinthewilderness.com** for more about these books (including their introduction, table of contents, and ordering information) and booklets.

The Coming of the King

in Matthew 24 and 25

Paul Cozza

A Place in the Wilderness

THE COMING OF THE KING
IN MATTHEW 24 AND 25

© 2023 Paul Cozza

ISBN 978-1-0881-3330-9

All rights reserved.
No part of this publication may be reproduced or transmitted in any form or by any means – electronic, mechanical, or any other, including photocopy, recording, or any information or retrieval system – without prior written consent, in hardcopy paper form, from:

Paul Cozza
A Place in the Wilderness

Email: paul@aplaceinthewilderness.com
Website: aplaceinthewilderness.com

Scripture quotations are from the American Standard Version of the Bible (1901) unless otherwise noted.

Cover design: Nuggitz Creative Services (Nuggitz.com)
Cover Photo: mycola_adams | DepositPhotos.com

Table of Contents

Preface 1
Introduction 3
Chapter 1 – The Preamble 7
   False Christs 8
   Wars 8
   Famines and Earthquakes 8
   Enduring to the End 9
   Warning, Enlightenment, and Encouragement 9
   The First Four Seals 10
Chapter 2 – Israel 11
   The Abomination of Desolation 11
   The Fifth Trumpet 13
   Further Suffering 14
   Flight 15
   Coming from Above 16
   Christ's Return in Glory 17
Chapter 3 – The Church 19
   The Living Believers 19
   One Taken, One Left 22
   Watch! 23
   Only the Father 25
   The Householder 26
   The Stewards 29
   The Virgins 31
   The Apostle's Word 35

  A Hidden Warning 36
  The Talents 37
  The Judgment Seat 39
Chapter 4 – The Nations **43**
Chapter 5 – A Further Word **47**
  A Specific Word 48
  The Early Church 48
  Yet Another Warning 52
Chapter 6 – A Pleased God **55**
  God's Desire 55
  God's Working 57
  A Window 59
  God Satisfied 60
Chapter 7 – One **63**
  Not Conformity 63
  Not a Human Leader 63
  Not a Set of Doctrines 64
  Not of Human Origin 64
  God Himself 64
  God's Working 65
  Our Part 67
  Layers 68
  Relationships 69
  Arriving 70
Chapter 8 - The Wisdom of God **71**
  Ruling 72
  A Proper Living 73
  God's Way 73
  The Wisdom of God 74

Chapter 9 – A Perfected Church 75
Recovery 76
The Lack 77
Deacons and Elders 78
God's Heart 79
God's Way 81
Life, Not Power 82
The Difference 82
A Comparison 83

Preface

I awoke early one morning—probably between 2 and 3 a.m.—with a pair of verses from Matthew 24 before my mind's eye. I saw something in those two verses that I had never noticed before, although I had read them perhaps hundreds of times. There was one particular word in each of the two verses that stood out, as if it were highlighted. I considered and wondered, *Why did the Lord use that word?* The Lord is always precise and accurate. He could have said what He did in several ways, yet He chose that particular word, and it bothered me. Why did He speak it that way?

I looked at the verses containing that word, first in one way, then in another. Then I looked at them in yet a third way. But no matter how I considered them, I came back to the same conclusion. I could see no other way to explain the Lord's choice of words. What is concealed there was completely unexpected; there was something precious hidden in plain sight. When these verses are fulfilled, as they will be by the end of this age, it will produce a life change for some. It will change how we live and how we interact. It will change our concepts, our desires, and our goals.

I pondered these two verses for months. I fellowshipped with others about what I was seeing, to perhaps discover some other explanation for the Lord's choice of words. However, each time I returned to that same inescapable conclusion. No one had a different, reasonable explanation for the Lord's choice of words.

I had no idea how to proceed with what I saw. What was before my eyes was intensely practical, yet I saw no way to practice what I was seeing. It was clear the Lord Himself would have to do something in His own mysterious and divine way. I had no way forward; I had no way to address many of the issues that arose from my understanding of these two verses. I wondered and considered, *Lord, how will You bring this about.* Eventually, I asked the Lord, "What do I do?" The Lord responded with one word: "Write!" And so, I write this book.

2 *The Coming of the King*

Introduction

The Gospel of Matthew depicts Christ as the King, coming to initiate, establish, and build His kingdom. It is crucial to understand Christ's kingdom is a kingdom of *life*. It is not a kingdom of manufactured behavior, but one of the divine life being lived out through those who believe into Him and receive Him.

Chapters 5-7 of Matthew show us the reality of this kingdom. These chapters depict how the life of God is manifested in His kingdom people. That life and its manifestation are the reality of the kingdom—that is, these chapters show what Christ's kingdom actually is in practice. Here we see God's life manifested practically. When someone strikes you on one cheek, you offer the other. Only God's life could do such a thing, could live in such a way. When someone wants to take your cloak, you offer your coat as well. Who but God could react in such a way? When someone hates, despises, and reviles you, you pray for him! You pray he might be brought into Christ's kingdom with all its riches and goodness. Such a reaction is not that of a natural person, but of a person indwelt by God, and through whom God flows and is seen. This is the reality of the kingdom as depicted in Matthew 5-7.

Matthew 13 reveals the appearance of the kingdom. Here we see what actually has happened during the last two millennia: Christ sowed the word of God as the seed of the kingdom, to impart the divine life into man—a seed that has been growing for about 2000 years. But during that growth, Christ's enemy has produced counterfeits, contaminants, and mutations in an attempt to frustrate God and destroy what Christ is building.

As Christ—the sower—sows Himself as the seed of the word into man, His enemy steals, starves, and stunts the growth of that seed. The hardened ground from which the evil one steals the seed, the rocks under the surface of men's hearts that starve the seed, and the thorns and thistles of daily life that stunt the growth of the seed—all are the evil devices of Christ's enemy.

As the seed of Christ's word grows, the enemy sows counterfeits among the wheat of God's crop. He sows tares that look nearly identical to wheat until the time of harvest, until they are fully exposed as false and of the evil one.

Then, as the pure flour of God's word spreads and feeds God's people, the enemy comes in to leaven, adulterate, and poison the truth in the word with falsehoods of various kinds.

Finally, as the herb—the mustard seed—of God's meek and lowly[1] life spreads over the Earth, the enemy mutates that herb into a tree, into something abnormal and not according to the life of that mustard seed. And in the branches of that tree, he lodges with his evil forces.

But despite this, the Lord gains the exceedingly precious pearl—the Church. He gains the treasure hidden in the field—the people of God, particularly the people of Israel. In addition, He gains the fish—the people at the end of this age from among the nations whom He judges worthy to enter His kingdom due to their proper behavior.

Then, in chapters 24-25, we see the coming of the King and the manifestation of the kingdom. These chapters greatly confuse many Christians. This confusion is often due to misapplying the verses in these chapters, and not realizing of whom the Lord is speaking. To understand these chapters clearly, we must understand the breadth of the Lord's word. In 24:3 the disciples ask for the sign of His presence and of the consummation of the age. The Lord's response is complex because the situation on the Earth is complex. To grasp these chapters, we must see there are three peoples on Earth.

Israel – the Jews

The Church – the genuine Christian believers

The Nations or the Gentiles – the remainder of humanity

In these chapters, the Lord answers the disciples' questions regarding all three of these peoples. To answer accurately, the

---

[1] Matt. 11:29

Lord must address each of these three peoples individually. The disciples had asked for the sign of His presence, and the Lord's answer is different for each of the three peoples.

Therefore, breaking down these two chapters properly, we have:

> **The Preamble** (Matthew 24:1-24:14) — This section is the preamble to this whole portion. In this section, the Lord describes what will occur before the end. By this, He prepares His disciples for the long church age and the suffering that will occur during it. He steels His disciples against the false promises of His coming. This section corresponds to the opening of the first four seals in the book of Revelation.
>
> **The Jews** (Matthew 24:15-24:30) — Many things happen to Israel at the end of the age, but the great sign of the Lord's presence to the Jews is the abomination of desolation. When that abomination is set up, it will indicate the Lord is very near, at the very doors.
>
> **The Church** (Matthew 24:36-25:30) — In this section, the Lord is answering the question concerning His presence with respect to the Church. Whereas the previous section related only to the Jews, this section relates only to the Church. However, to the Church there are no specific signs! As it was in the days of Noah—when people were buying, selling, marrying, and giving in marriage—so it will be to the Church at the end of this age. Everything will seem to be proceeding as it always has. But in the midst of this, the Lord comes for the believers—for the *watchful* believers.
>
> **The Nations** (Matthew 25:31-25:46) — There is also no sign to the nations except the Lord's physical coming in glory. At that time, He will judge the nations according to how they treated His brothers during the last years of this age. Those who treated His brothers properly will be blessed to enter into the eternal life of His kingdom.

If we see these portions clearly, it will greatly simplify this otherwise complex section of Matthew. With such an understanding, these chapters are much easier to parse, our confusion is limited, and our understanding is greatly enhanced. With this as a background, let us now examine Matthew 24-25.

CHAPTER 1

The Preamble

And as he sat on the mount of Olives, the disciples came unto him privately, saying, Tell us, when shall these things be? and what shall be the sign of thy coming, and of the end of the world? And Jesus answered and said unto them, Take heed that no man lead you astray. For many shall come in my name, saying, I am the Christ; and shall lead many astray. And ye shall hear of wars and rumors of wars; see that ye be not troubled: for these things must needs come to pass; but the end is not yet. For nation shall rise against nation, and kingdom against kingdom; and there shall be famines and earthquakes in divers places. But all these things are the beginning of travail. Then shall they deliver you up unto tribulation, and shall kill you: and ye shall be hated of all the nations for my name's sake. And then shall many stumble, and shall deliver up one another, and shall hate one another. And many false prophets shall arise, and shall lead many astray. And because iniquity shall be multiplied, the love of the many shall wax cold. But he that endureth to the end, the same shall be saved. And this gospel of the kingdom shall be preached in the whole world for a testimony unto all the nations; and then shall the end come. (Matt. 24:3-14)

    The disciples ask the Lord what the sign of His presence and of the consummation of the age would be. Before answering, the Lord provides a preamble, an introductory word, telling His disciples what would come to pass before the end of the age. Although the disciples did not know it, between the time of their question and the end of the age would be about 2000 years, during which many things would occur. The Lord addresses these matters first, as a preparation to His disciples and all the believers who would follow them, indicating what would happen during the intervening church age.

False Christs

There would be many false christs. Who can say over the last 2000 years how many have appeared pretending to be from God, attempting to usurp Christ's position, and in some cases even pretending to be Christ Himself? There have been John Smith and the Mormons, Mohammed and the Muslims, various gurus in India and elsewhere. Who can say how many false ones have arisen? The Lord's word is true and has come to pass.

Wars

The Lord spoke of wars and rumors of wars. Nation would rise up against nation, and kingdom against kingdom. Consider: how many wars have there been since the Lord walked the Earth? In but our own time there have been scores: Korea, Vietnam, Iran, Iraq, Bosnia, Afghanistan, Israel, and numerous others. Indeed, the time from the Lord's word until now has been marked by war—civil, nation against nation, and kingdom against kingdom.

Famines and Earthquakes

The Lord also says there would be famines and earthquakes in various places. Over the centuries, consider how many famines there have been. From the great medieval famines in Europe, China, Russia, India, and elsewhere, to the many great famines in more modern times, to the many lesser famines, humanity has been suffering these disasters from the time of the Lord until the present. And how many earthquakes have shaken the Earth over the last two millennia? Great earthquakes,[1] such as the ones in Chile, Alaska, Indonesia, Japan, and elsewhere, and innumerable smaller quakes have repeatedly shaken the Earth.

All of these have been occurring from the time of the apostles until now, and will continue. However, the end is not yet. We should not be distracted or troubled by all of these happenings,

---

[1] These earthquakes should not be confused with the four great earthquakes that shake the Earth during the endtime and are recorded in the book of Revelation (Rev. 6:12, 8:5, 11:13, 11:19/16:18).

for they are not indicative of the Lord's imminent return. All of these are but the beginning of travail. When the end comes, it will be far, far worse.

Enduring to the End

Furthermore, the apostles and the Lord's disciples would be delivered up to tribulation and death. Hate would predominate. False prophets would arise in abundance. Lawlessness and sinfulness would not only abound, but be multiplied. And in the midst of such evils—hate, lawlessness, and sinfulness—the love of many would grow cold.

Here, the Lord grants an encouraging word: the one who endures to the end will be saved. Of what "end" is the Lord speaking? The end of the age? The end of one's life? I believe the Lord is encouraging us to endure until the end of whatever trials God has assigned to us. Our endurance through such trials works out our own salvation. We should not run from trials, but embrace those the Lord has assigned to us. God causes them all to work together for our good.[1]

All of these great tumults will occur repeatedly before the end, for it is not until this gospel of the kingdom is preached to the entire inhabited Earth that the end will come.

Warning, Enlightenment, and Encouragement

As we consider the Lord's word in response to His disciples' question, we can see that He begins by offering words of warning, enlightenment, and encouragement. He warns of false christs and prophets—not just once, but twice, indicating the seriousness of the threat from these false ones. He warns of wars and calamities of various kinds. By this, He settles the hearts of His disciples concerning what is to come. He prepares them to pass through the travail of their lives on Earth. He also warns of a time of great iniquity. We are certainly in such a time, a time when good is called evil and evil called good, a time of enormous

---

[1] Rom. 8:28

deception, immorality, and hatred. The Lord speaks all these words to help keep the disciples' hearts warm and loving.

The Lord's speaking is also an enlightenment. He does not leave us in the dark regarding what would occur during the time of His physical absence. Such enlightenment safeguards us in the midst of turmoil. It is a kind of bedrock upon which our lives can be built and stand during a storm. We know what must come to pass, and consequently are not surprise or distressed when we see these things occur. We know, for example, that great iniquity would come—and, in fact, is already here.

His words are also an encouragement. Should we endure to the end, should we pass through all the difficulties and troubles that will beset us—especially the evil and persecution directed towards the Christian believers—we will be saved. This is not to be saved from the lake of fire, into which many unbelievers will be cast. This is to be saved from the kind of person we are within, from our own fallen nature and natural being. Through our endurance, we are changed within to be like Him. This is the greatest salvation! This word helps keep our hearts warm, opened, and full of love toward the Lord.

The First Four Seals

This passage in Matthew corresponds to the opening of the first four seals[1] in the book of Revelation. There we see four horsemen who represent, in order, the gospel, war, famine, and pestilence with death. These depict in a general way the events from the time of the Lord's ascension until the end, just as this passage in Matthew does. The gospel has gone out to reach the ends of the Earth; war has broken out across the Earth, no doubt in a Satanic attempt to frustrate the gospel; the result of these wars is famine; famine and other pestilences cause death. Both the portions here in Matthew and in Revelation are a brief overview of the last 2000 years.

---

[1] Rev. 6:1-8

CHAPTER 2

Israel

The Lord's introductory word set the stage for His answer to the disciples' question. The Lord answers the disciples' question for each of the three peoples on Earth—Israel, the Church, and the Nations—in turn, because His answer differs according to which of the three He is referring. First, in verses 15-35, He addresses the Jews. If these verses were to be applied to the Church, it would lead to much confusion. This section of the Word refers only to Israel, as indicated by the Lord's reference to Judea in verse 16 and to the tribes of Israel in verse 30.

The Abomination of Desolation

When therefore ye see the abomination of desolation, which was spoken of through Daniel the prophet, standing in the holy place (let him that readeth understand), then let them that are in Judaea flee unto the mountains: let him that is on the housetop not go down to take out the things that are in his house: and let him that is in the field not return back to take his cloak. But woe unto them that are with child and to them that give suck in those days! And pray ye that your flight be not in the winter, neither on a sabbath: for then shall be great tribulation, such as hath not been from the beginning of the world until now, no, nor ever shall be. (Matt. 24:15-21)

The disciples asked what the sign of the Lord's presence and of the consummation of the age would be. For the Jews, that sign will be the *abomination of desolation* being set up in the holy place, as spoken of by the prophet Daniel.[1] This abomination is the idol spoken of in Revelation 13.[2] When this is set up in the Jewish Temple—which has not, as yet, been constructed—it will indicate the Lord is present and the end near.

At that time, those in Judea should flee to the mountains.[3] These fleeing ones must be the Jewish believers in Israel: they alone would be familiar with the warning in these verses and have the faith to follow the Lord's instruction. These should be the 144,000 of Israel who are sealed at the opening of the sixth seal mentioned in the book of Revelation,[4] and the ones who have seen the visions and dreamt the dreams of the endtime as revealed in the book of Joel.[5] They will know of this warning, believe this word, and flee to the mountains. The remaining Jews—the unbelieving in Israel—will stay behind to pass through the great suffering that is about to happen. This will take place about two to three years before the Lord's physical return to the Earth.

It is *then* that there will be great tribulation *in Israel*. While this phrase—the great tribulation—is often used to refer to the immense suffering through which the whole Earth will pass during the endtime, it actually refers to that part of the endtime when Israel suffers greatly. The great tribulation is something *Israel* passes through. What the whole Earth passes through is called *the*

---

[1] Here the Lord inserts the phrase, *let him that readeth understand*. Understand what? The Lord had just mentioned Daniel. By inserting this word, the Lord is verifying that Daniel, as depicted in his book, is real and the book he wrote authentic, unlike what many false ones say about Daniel to mislead people. The Lord's word indicates that Daniel is a prophet and that his prophecies are true. Furthermore, it also means the Temple must be rebuilt before the Lord's return, because the Lord said the abomination will stand in the *holy place*. There is only one such holy place in the Jewish religion—the inner chamber of the Temple.

[2] Rev. 13:15-17

[3] This should refer to the mountains to the north in Israel, perhaps in what is called the Golan Heights. The mountains to the east of Israel remain in the hands of the Arabs. It is unlikely they would welcome Jews fleeing persecution in Israel!

[4] Rev. 7:1-8

[5] Joel 2:28-29

hour of trial.[1] This great tribulation to Israel is also called the time of Jacob's trouble[2] and the time of trouble.[3] It is described in some detail in chapters 9 and 13 of Revelation.

The Fifth Trumpet

And the fifth angel sounded, and I saw a star from heaven fallen unto the earth: and there was given to him the key of the pit of the abyss. And he opened the pit of the abyss; and there went up a smoke out of the pit, as the smoke of a great furnace; and the sun and the air were darkened by reason of the smoke of the pit. And out of the smoke came forth locusts upon the earth; and power was given them, as the scorpions of the earth have power. And it was said unto them that they should not hurt the grass of the earth, neither any green thing, neither any tree, but only such men as have not the seal of God on their foreheads. And it was given them that they should not kill them, but that they should be tormented five months: and their torment was as the torment of a scorpion, when it striketh a man. And in those days men shall seek death, and shall in no wise find it; and they shall desire to die, and death fleeth from them. And the shapes of the locusts were like unto horses prepared for war; and upon their heads as it were crowns like unto gold, and their faces were as men's faces. And they had hair as the hair of women, and their teeth were as the teeth of lions. And they had breastplates, as it were breastplates of iron; and the sound of their wings was as the sound of chariots, of many horses rushing to war. And they have tails like unto scorpions, and stings; and in their tails is their power to hurt men five months. They have over them as king the angel of the abyss: his name in Hebrew is Abaddon, and in the Greek tongue he hath the name Apollyon. (Rev. 9:1-11)

When the fifth trumpet sounds, an angel—no doubt Satan—opens the shaft of the abyss. That is, he provides a way for the

---

[1] Rev. 3:10

[2] Jer. 30:7

[3] Dan. 12:1

demonic spirits held beneath the Earth to escape to the Earth's surface. They are likened to locusts, and rising from the abyss with them is their king, who is called Abaddon and Apollyon.[1] A description of the Antichrist's armies in Israel follows, indicating his armies will be demon-possessed during the endtime.

John the apostle saw the actual events that will transpire in Israel, but he had no way to adequately describe what he was seeing. Our modern-day technology was unknown to him. He had no words to define the weapons he saw, the types of body armor the forces will be wearing, or the vehicles then being used. So, he described them in the words of his time.

These forces will have some sort of weapon which causes intense pain—pain so great that those struck by this weapon would rather die. However, death will flee from them. This is the beginning of the great tribulation in Israel—Israel's initial suffering. This will last for five months.

Further Suffering

And I saw another beast coming up out of the earth; and he had two horns like unto a lamb, and he spake as a dragon. And he exerciseth all the authority of the first beast in his sight. And he maketh the earth and them that dwell therein to worship the first beast, whose death-stroke was healed. And he doeth great signs, that he should even make fire to come down out of heaven upon the earth in the sight of men. And he deceiveth them that dwell on the earth by reason of the signs which it was given him to do in the sight of the beast; saying to them that dwell on the earth, that they should make an image to the beast who hath the stroke of the sword and lived. And it was given unto him to give breath to it, even to the image of the beast, that the image of the beast should both speak, and cause that as many as should not worship the image of the beast should be killed. And he causeth all, the small and the great, and the rich and the poor, and the free and the bond,

---

[1] Apollyon/Abaddon should refer to the spirit of Caesar Nero, who will inhabit the body of the Antichrist after he is slain (Rev. 17:8-11). This will cause the dead Antichrist to appear to be resurrected.

that there be given them a mark on their right hand, or upon their forehead; and that no man should be able to buy or to sell, save he that hath the mark, even the name of the beast or the number of his name. Here is wisdom. He that hath understanding, let him count the number of the beast; for it is the number of a man: and his number is Six hundred and sixty and six. (Rev. 13:11-18)

After that initial time of torment, even more suffering will beset Israel. This is depicted in Revelation 13. The leader of Israel at that time will be a "beast" allied with the Antichrist. That leader will attempt to coerce every person in Israel to receive the mark of the Antichrist. This should be no ordinary mark on the skin, but something technological that allows that leader to control those bearing the mark. The ones who refuse the mark will not be able to buy or sell. Many will hunger in those days.

Furthermore, the Jews will be compelled to worship the image—the abomination of desolation. Those who refuse will be subjected to death or exiled as slaves. The slaughter of the Jews in Israel will be immense and unfathomable.

Flight

… then let them that are in Judaea flee unto the mountains: let him that is on the housetop not go down to take out the things that are in his house: and let him that is in the field not return back to take his cloak. But woe unto them that are with child and to them that give suck in those days! And pray ye that your flight be not in the winter, neither on a sabbath: for then shall be great tribulation, such as hath not been from the beginning of the world until now, no, nor ever shall be. And except those days had been shortened, no flesh would have been saved: but for the elect's sake those days shall be shortened. (Matt. 24:16-22)

For those Jews who flee to the mountains, their flight must be immediate. To turn back for anything is to risk being caught in the great suffering Israel will have to endure. This will be the worst suffering there has ever been or will ever be again. There has never been anything like it, nor will there be. If we look back upon what has transpired in Jewish history—not to mention all human history—this word is soul-shaking. Consider what happened to the Jews when Nebuchadnezzar overran Israel and destroyed Jerusalem in 587 BC. Look at what the Romans did to Israel and Jerusalem in 70 AD, when they did not leave one stone of the temple upon another. Consider the unspeakable slaughter and heart-wrenching horror of World War II. This future time will be worse than all of these to Israel. In fact, if the Lord does not cut short that time by His physical return, no flesh will survive. It is not that no *Jews* would survive, but that not a single *human being* would remain alive.

Coming from Above

Then if any man shall say unto you, Lo, here is the Christ, or, Here; believe it not. For there shall arise false Christs, and false prophets, and shall show great signs and wonders; so as to lead astray, if possible, even the elect. Behold, I have told you beforehand. If therefore they shall say unto you, Behold, he is in the wilderness; go not forth: Behold, he is in the inner chambers; believe it not. For as the lightning cometh forth from the east, and is seen even unto the west; so shall be the coming of the Son of man. Wheresoever the carcase is, there will the eagles be gathered together. (Matt. 24:23-28)

During those years, many false prophets will arise in Israel. The worst of these is the second beast mentioned in the last half of Revelation 13. He presents himself as a lamb, but speaks like a dragon. All these false prophets try to mislead God's elect, even though that is not possible. They try to persuade God's elect from among the Jews to go into the inner chambers[1] to find the Messiah. They also attempt to persuade them to go into the wilderness for the Messiah. But the Lord will come from above. He will break through the great darkness covering the world, and like the lightning shining from the east to the west, will illuminate the whole Earth with His glory. By this, He will cut short those days of suffering. He will end the multinational assault upon Israel, and

---

[1] The inner chambers here may refer to the spot where the abomination stands.

then dispose of everyone and everything offensive to His kingdom.

Christ's Return in Glory

But immediately after the tribulation of those days the sun shall be darkened, and the moon shall not give her light, and the stars shall fall from heaven, and the powers of the heavens shall be shaken: and then shall appear the sign of the Son of man in heaven: and then shall all the tribes of the earth mourn, and they shall see the Son of man coming on the clouds of heaven with power and great glory. And he shall send forth his angels with a great sound of a trumpet, and they shall gather together his elect from the four winds, from one end of heaven to the other. Now from the fig tree learn her parable: when her branch is now become tender, and putteth forth its leaves, ye know that the summer is nigh; even so ye also, when ye see all these things, know ye that he is nigh, even at the doors. Verily I say unto you, This generation shall not pass away, till all these things be accomplished. Heaven and earth shall pass away, but my words shall not pass away. (Matt. 24:29-35)

The great tribulation will last quite a long time—about two to three years, then it will suddenly stop. There will be signs in the heavens: numerous meteors, and the sun and moon not giving off light. Then Israel will see the sign of the Son of man above. Some have speculated this will be a cross of some sort, and it very well may be. Seeing this, all those left in Israel will realize their great sin in rejecting Christ. They will mourn and repent. It is then that the Lord will part the heavens and return in glory physically. However, the Lord's physical return in glory is only for Israel and the nations, not for the believers. There is much confusion about this. For the believers the Lord's return will be hidden, not outward; for Israel and the nations the Lord's return will be physically in glory.

When these things happen, the Lord is near, at the very doors. He is about to appear. Indeed, this current age of evil, in which we are now, will not pass away until all things spoken by the Lord are fulfilled. Heaven and Earth will pass away, but the

Lord's word will never pass away. His word is true. What He speaks comes to pass.

CHAPTER 3

The Church

The Lord's speaking regarding the Church in these chapters of Matthew is comparatively long, extending from 24:36 to 25:30. Whereas the previous section spoke of Israel alone during the endtime, this section concerns only the believers. It is broken into three parts. The first, from 24:36 to 24:51, addresses those believers alive on the Earth at the time of the Lord's return. The second, from 25:1 to 25:13, talks of the believers who have died before the Lord's coming. The final section, from 25:14 to 25:30, is a general word spoken to all believers, whether they have died before the Lord's coming or are living at that time.

The Living Believers

But of that day and hour knoweth no one, not even the angels of heaven, neither the Son, but the Father only. And as were the days of Noah, so shall be the coming of the Son of man. For as in those days which were before the flood they were eating and drinking, marrying and giving in marriage, until the day that Noah entered into the ark, and they knew not until the flood came, and took them all away; so shall be the coming of the Son of man. Then shall two men be in the field; one is taken, and one is left: two women shall be grinding at the mill; one is taken, and one is left. Watch therefore: for ye know not on what day your Lord cometh. (Matt. 24:36-42)

Interestingly, the Lord gives no sign of His presence when speaking of the believers. Indeed, He tells us that everything will be proceeding as if nothing out of the ordinary was about to happen: people will be eating and drinking, marrying and giving in marriage, just as in Noah's day. And just as it was in Noah's day—when Noah entered the ark, God's judgment came—so will it be at the end of the age. When the watchful believers are taken, God's judgment and the end of the age will come.

The reason The Lord gives no sign is that when He comes for the believers, He will come as a thief. He will come secretly to "steal" them away from this world. He tells us explicitly, of that day and hour no one knows—no man, no angel, not even the Son—except the Father alone. It is a moment hidden in the Father. When the Lord comes, no one will be expecting His return in such a hidden way. But once this happens, then the Lord's presence among the believers will be manifested and the end of the age will be at hand.

Many Christians believe that the ones taken in Matthew 24:40-41 are believers and the ones left are unbelievers. They come to this conclusion based upon their belief that all Christians will be taken before the endtime upheavals come. According to such an understanding, being born again is sufficient to be taken. There is no consideration of the maturity of the believer in the divine life, nor of the relationship between Christ and the believer. They believe it is sufficient simply to have been born again. But let us examine these verses with a sober mind, unbiased by any preconceived notions or doctrines.

It should be clear these verses include both encouragement and warning. However, we must ask, a warning to whom? The unbelievers do not read the Bible. If all the believers are taken at that time and the unbelievers don't read the Bible, then to whom is the Lord addressing these words? This whole section must be for believers; otherwise it is a meaningless warning.

In this section, the Lord commands—*commands*—to watch. Whom is He commanding? The unbelievers do not know about this command, nor would they care even if they did. Furthermore, if all the Christians are taken before the end comes, why would the Lord command at all? The Lord's words in the Gospel of Mark[1] are even stronger: *What I say unto you, I say unto all: Watch!* How could the Lord's words be more clear? He tells all to watch.

---

[1] Mark 13:37

Certainly the word "all" includes all the believers. Why would He tell the believers to watch if all of them are taken before the end?

In the Gospel of Luke,[1] the Lord's words are even more precise: *But watch ye at every season, making supplication, that ye may prevail to escape all these things that shall come to pass, and to stand before the Son of man.* We must always watch and pray in order that we might prevail—might be accounted worthy—to escape all these things that shall come to pass. In other words, those who do not watch and pray will not escape all the things coming upon the Earth. They will pass through the great endtime sufferings that will come upon the whole inhabited Earth.

The Lord also commands His disciples to be ready. Since we do not know the hour in which the Lord returns, we must always be ready for His return. How could this word, spoken by the Lord to His disciples, be for unbelievers? What unbeliever will ever be ready for the Lord's return? And to emphasize this point, in the next chapter of Matthew the Lord goes on to say that those who are *ready* will go in with Him to His marriage feast.[2] After they enter, the door to that feast will be shut. Those who are not ready, who are not prepared for the Lord's return, who have not watched and prayed, who have not lived a life in contact with the Lord, will not go into the marriage feast. Rather, they will be shut out of that feast during the coming age. All these words in Matthew are serious and sobering. We must not dismiss them as not being applicable to ourselves, as if they applied to someone else.

It is absolutely paramount for us to see that in Matthew 24:40-41, both those who are taken and those who are left behind are believers. Seeing this will motivate us to watch. Believing otherwise may damage our Christian walk, for if we believe all born-again Christians are taken at that time, then there is no need for us to do anything. If the Lord takes all believers, we have no need to mature in the divine life or to faithfully serve the Lord while here on Earth. It should be clear that this kind of

---

[1] Luke 21:36

[2] Matt. 25:10

unpreparedness is something of the evil one, something the evil one desires. In short, these verses in this whole section of Matthew are to the believers.

One Taken, One Left

When the Lord comes for the believers, He will do so secretly. When He comes for Israel, He does so openly, from the heavens. But when He comes for the believers, He comes secretly, as a thief. He does not come openly from above; rather, He comes secretly from *within*. The Christ who is coming for the believers is coming from within us![1]

At that time—that incredible moment—He will call us to Himself, perhaps by merely speaking our name. Those who love Him above all else will respond by simply going with Him. They will be taken along[2] as He—the heavenly thief—gathers all that is precious to Him. He will be the heavenly transport to bring the watchful and prepared believers to stand before their Father in glory. How we should long for that moment, leaving all that is not God behind and becoming one with Him in the fullest of ways! Every Christian should have such a heart, longing to be with Christ before our Father. This is our eternal station.

But we must ask, to what is our heart attached? Is it attached to Christ only? What will happen if our heart turns to something else when He calls us to Himself? Perhaps our heart will turn to our spouse, whom we so dearly love. If so, we will be left behind. Perhaps it will turn to our children. If so, we will be left behind. Perhaps our heart will turn to something of the world—to sports, to amusements, to our job, or even to something religious. If so, we will be left behind. At that moment, if our heart turns from Christ to anything, it will be too late. *We will be left behind.* Remember Lot's wife. She turned back and became a pillar of salt, a monument to the shame of turning from the Lord back to something she held to be more dear.

---

[1] Col. 3:4

[2] The Greek word here means not simply *take*, but *take along* or *take with*.

We may say that the Lord Himself is most important to us. But, in numerous instances, this is not true. We say that, but our heart knows differently: we love something more than Him; we are attached to something besides Him. At His coming there will be only the Lord, we, and our real heart condition. Wherever our heart really is, there we will turn. Whatever our heart really loves, really cherishes, really desires, there our heart will turn. There will be no deception or delusion; there will be no faking our true condition; there will be no concealing what and how we really are. What and how we really are will be brought into the light by our reaction in that instant. If the Lord calls us this very second, to where does our heart turn?

The Lord will come in an hour that we think not. He will come at a most unexpected time. There will be no way to prepare some kind of false presentation for that moment, for not only will we not know when, but we also will not expect it. At that time, only we and our real condition will be before the Lord. We will be taken or left according to what we have become by that time.

Two men will be in the field and two women will be grinding at the mill. They will be going about their normal daily lives. They will have no expectation that everything is about to change. Then, instantly, everything will change! Whether for good—to stand before the Father, or for bad—to pass through the judgments coming upon the whole Earth, that moment will declare the truth: the truth about us, the truth about our condition, the truth about how we have spent our lives, our time, and our energy during our Christian life.

Watch!

The Lord has no desire that any of His children would pass through the great upheavals, turmoils, and sufferings of the end-time. He desires each one to be ready for the moment of His coming. Consequently, He commands us all to watch, for He knows that by watching we will become prepared.

What does it mean to watch? It means to be attentive to and to guard. What are we to be attentive to and guard? Our heart! We are to be attentive to our real inward condition before the Lord. We are to guard our heart from all entanglements. The world is too subtle, too deceptive, too insidious. There is something in the world to appeal to every human condition and desire. There is something created by the evil one to attract every human heart and distract it from God. The evil one knows how to deceive. He uses the world for this. We are to guard ourselves from worldly entanglements, from worldly attachments. The whole world lies in the evil one.[1] We must know this, believe it, and guard ourselves from it. This is to watch.

To watch also means to stay awake. Recall what the apostle said:[2] *Awake, thou that sleepest, and arise from the dead, and Christ shall shine upon thee.* To watch is also to be awake before the Lord, to have our inward eyes open. It is to have the eyes of our heart open to the One who is shining within and upon us. It is to be watching Him moment by moment. Recall 2 Corinthians:[3] *But we all, with unveiled face beholding as in a mirror the glory of the Lord, are transformed into the same image from glory to glory, even as from the Lord the Spirit.* We must have no veil of sleep upon our heart. Our spiritual eyes must be open and seeing, not closed and blind.

We now can see why the Lord commands us to watch. On the one hand, it protects us from the evil one's devices. On the other hand, it opens us up to the shining of the Lord Himself, which transforms us from what we once were into His very image. It is those who bear His image that will be taken in that day.

In all this there is something of great importance: we must have a single eye for the Lord. We must have a heart set upon Him, set upon the things above—God, Christ, and God's purpose. We must have a heart for God—loving Him, desiring Him, and wanting Him above all else. Remember the Lord's word:[4] *The lamp of the body is the eye: if therefore thine eye be single, thy*

---

[1] 1 John 5:19

[2] Eph. 5:14

[3] 2 Cor. 3:18

[4] Matt. 6:22-23

whole body shall be full of light. But if thine eye be evil, thy whole body shall be full of darkness. If therefore the light that is in thee be darkness, how great is the darkness!

Only the Father

No one knows of that day and hour except the Father—no man, no angel, and not even the Son of God Himself! The Father in His wisdom withholds that knowledge. He withholds it from us and from the angels. But how could the Father, who is God, withhold this from the Son, who is also God? This is a mystery. It may be that the Father, for His particular and wonderful purposes, asks the Son not to look into that time to discern the day and hour. And it may be that the Son, even though He is God, honors the Father by not looking. How sweet this is!

None of us knows the hour of the Lord's coming. But, as described below in the parable of the householder, the Lord says that if we knew the time of His coming, we would watch. A logical question then is, if we would watch if we knew the hour, why not tell us? God wants all believers to watch, even those who will have died by the time of the Lord's return. If we knew that the Lord was not returning for, say, another thousand years, that might be a disincentive to some. If His coming is decades, centuries, or even millennia away, we might feel no urgency to prepare for His return.

But why does He not tell the angels? If the angels knew, Satan would also know. He could use that information to try to interfere with the interaction between the Lord and the believers at the moment of His secret coming. When the Lord comes secretly for us, there will be only He and we in our true condition. If Satan knew of that time, he might try to distract us in some way at that very moment. That moment is precious, and not something for Satan. When that moment comes, even Satan will be surprised. How marvelous that is!

The Father does not even tell His Son. The Lord's task is to bring all of God's people to maturity in the divine life, and this task is ongoing. There is no single moment at which all of God's sons mature together. At one point, the firstfruits are reaped; at a later point, the harvest. It is the Father who will decide when to reap the firstfruits, according to their maturity. This will happen when He, Himself, is satisfied.

I also believe that the Father withholds this information from His Son as a kind of exquisite surprise blessing. From the time of His ascension, Jesus has been working to bring all the believers to maturity as full-grown sons of God to stand before our Father in glory. We have such an elder brother who is doing this for us and for our Father. The Father, in His time, will announce to the Son the completion of the first stage of the Son's task. The Father will say, "Now!" and the Son will come for the believers, bringing with Him all who have matured to be firstfruits to the Father for His deep satisfaction. Could there be a scene more sweet, more precious, more dear, and more excellent?

The Householder

But know this, that if the master of the house had known in what watch the thief was coming, he would have watched, and would not have suffered his house to be broken through. Therefore be ye also ready; for in an hour that ye think not the Son of man cometh. (Matt. 24:43-44)

The Lord then speaks a brief parable to help us see the seriousness of His command to watch. He says if the master of the house—the householder—knew at what time of the night[1] the thief was coming, he would watch and not allow his house to be broken into. There are several points in this short parable that are of importance. We must understand that we are the householders and the Lord is the thief coming to steal what is precious to Him. If we knew the Lord was coming as a thief, and the approximate time of His return, we would watch for that time in order to be ready for the Lord's secret coming. For example, if we knew the

---

[1] The Jewish day of the Lord's time was divided into a day of about 12 hours and a night of 4 watches. The Lord said that He is coming as a thief during one of the night watches, indicating that since the time of His ascension we have been living in a kind of night. We have been in the darkness of Satan's activity and deception. We are now certainly in the fourth, or last, watch of that night, and the day of the Lord's coming is near.

Lord was coming secretly on May 3, 2032, to take to Himself what He deems precious, we would watch and prepare for that time. Since we do not know the time, He commands us to always watch so that we will be ready, regardless of when He comes.

The Lord's actual words in this parable are that the householder would not allow his house to be *dug through*. What does this mean, and how can we keep the Lord from *digging through* our house? The Lord's use of the word "dug" tells us the secret. If the Lord can dig through a house, that house must be made of earth or clay of some sort. However, by being watchful, by being awake to the Lord, by being conscious of His presence and looking to Him, we are changed.[1] We are transformed from something earthen to something priceless. If we are watchful, when the Lord comes as a thief to steal what is precious to Him, there then would be nothing to dig through! There would only be us—transformed, which He deems most precious.

If we are not watchful, then the Lord in His coming will expose our real and pitiful condition. His coming within us will shine to expose what we really are: earthen and not heavenly, fallen and not sanctified within, common and not transformed. In His coming, He will dig through the many layers of our protective defenses that previously have kept the Lord from touching our heart and exposing how we truly are, in order that we might be changed.

It is the Lord's desire that we all become precious to God, that we all gain Christ[2] in every part of our being. But we have many means by which we protect ourselves from His shining, exposing, operating, and transforming. We may have the habit of repeatedly excusing both our actions and what we are. By excusing ourselves before the Lord, we prevent His words from touching us and keep His light from shining within. Or we may turn away from Him whenever He comes as light to help us. Whether we turn in fear, in anger, in pride, or for some other reason, we are nevertheless refusing Him the permission to touch

---

[1] 2 Cor. 3:18

[2] Phil. 3:8

us within. Or we may talk incessantly. By doing so, we keep our heart untouched. We are so consumed with our own talking that we cannot hear. We cannot hear the words of others, and we cannot hear the words of the Lord. Consequently, our heart remains untouched and our person untransformed. Speaking too much is a means of preventing the Lord from touching our heart.

We may be proud and haughty. An arrogant person cannot receive the truth about his condition. Look at the Lord's word to the church in Laodicea.[1] There, the Lord tells the believers in Laodicea that they think they are rich and have need of nothing. But in reality, they are poor, blind, wretched, miserable, and naked. The pride in the believers there not only keeps them from the knowledge of their condition, but more importantly, keeps them from the Lord Himself. The Lord councils them to pay the price to gain *Him*: as gold that they may be truly rich, as white garments that they may be truly clothed, and as eyesalve that they may truly see. Pride, arrogance, and haughtiness are yet one more way by which we prevent the Lord from touching us.

However, when the Lord returns, He will "dig" through all these layers of defense. His coming from within us will expose everything. We will see our pride for what it is; we will hate our excuses for having kept us in our pitiful condition; we will despise our incessant talking, which prevented the Lord from enriching us; we will hate our habit of turning from the Lord when He came to us in His humility to help. It is crucial that we see and understand these matters; otherwise we may very well be unprepared for the Lord when He comes.

The way the verses in this parable are commonly translated leaves the impression that when the Lord comes for us, He will come from outside of us. The phrase "broken into" implies that. However, this is not the case. As mentioned above, the Lord actually said "dug through," not "broken into." When the Lord comes for the believers, He will actually come from within us. And so Paul says in Colossians,[2] *When Christ who is our life shall*

---

[1] Rev. 3:17-18

[2] Col. 3:4

appear, then shall we appear with Him in glory. Where is the Christ who is our life? Not in the heavens, but within us. When the Christ who is our life within comes forth from us, that is His secret coming for the believers. If we are prepared for that moment—for His coming from within, then we will be manifested with Him in glory by being fully taken from this earthly realm to the spiritual, heavenly realm to stand with Christ before the Father. But for those believers who are not prepared for His coming, He will *dig through* all the layers upon their heart from within, exposing their true condition, and leaving them behind to pass through the endtime trials.

The Stewards

Who then is the faithful and wise servant, whom his lord hath set over his household, to give them their food in due season? Blessed is that servant, whom his lord when he cometh shall find so doing. Verily I say unto you, that he will set him over all that he hath. But if that evil servant shall say in his heart, My lord tarrieth; and shall begin to beat his fellow-servants, and shall eat and drink with the drunken; the lord of that servant shall come in a day when he expecteth not, and in an hour when he knoweth not, and shall cut him asunder, and appoint his portion with the hypocrites: there shall be the weeping and the gnashing of teeth. (Matt. 24:45-51)

The Lord continues with a particular word to those among the believers who have been assigned the oversight of God's household. That is mainly a matter of nourishing God's people with the proper food at the proper time. Some among the believers have been gifted with a special portion of the Spirit to feed God's people with His divine word. But with that gift comes responsibility.

If a believer has the gift from the Lord to feed others, he must do so. Consider what the apostle Paul said: *Woe is me if I preach not the gospel.*[1] Paul had been given the gift to speak God's word for the building up of the Church. In exercising that gift, he

---

[1] 1 Cor. 9:16

not only brought numerous unbelievers to Christ, but also raised up multiple churches. This all came about through his speaking. For those who are so gifted, the same is true: woe to those who speak not the word of God! When the Lord returns, if He finds His steward feeding His people, the Lord will bless him with the highest service—He will set him over all that He has. How blessed is the faithful steward!

Some, although gifted in this same way, will think the Lord has delayed His coming. They will begin to eat and drink with the drunken, and to beat their fellow believers. This does not mean physically abusing others, although it certainly would include that. The beating here refers to some kind of coercion being carried out against the saints to force them into a certain mode of behavior. It includes berating, despising, belittling, demeaning, bullying, and slandering them. At His return, the Lord will recompense with severe discipline this kind of shameful, improper behavior by those who should be feeding God's people. Some of the Lord's stewards will feed; some will beat. Beating is the antithesis of feeding.

When the Lord returns and finds some of His stewards beating the saints, He will apportion grave punishment to them. He will cut them apart. This is not a physical killing, since even after being cut apart, they are assigned a portion with the hypocrites. Rather, this is a cutting into the heart, exposing the hidden evil that prompts such a shameful treatment of God's people. Then these will be assigned a portion with the hypocrites. What exactly that is, the Lord does not say. However, consider who the hypocrites are and what they will be experiencing after the Lord's return. To the shameful steward, the thousand-year reign of Christ, which should be a joy to all the saints, will be a time of intense suffering.

The Lord assigns these believers their portion with the hypocrites because that is what they also are—hypocrites. While outwardly they may present a godly and spiritual façade, inwardly they have a haughty heart, regarding themselves as superior. This kind of evil heart results in them mistreating the saints. This is a most serious warning. It is not simply to be left behind to pass through the suffering of the last three and a half years of this age, which many will have to experience. No, this is to be cut apart and assigned a share of what the godless hypocrites will experience. This is exceedingly serious.

The Virgins

Then shall the kingdom of heaven be likened unto ten virgins, who took their lamps, and went forth to meet the bridegroom. And five of them were foolish, and five were wise. For the foolish, when they took their lamps, took no oil with them: but the wise took oil in their vessels with their lamps. Now while the bridegroom tarried, they all slumbered and slept. But at midnight there is a cry, Behold, the bridegroom! Come ye forth to meet him. Then all those virgins arose, and trimmed their lamps. And the foolish said unto the wise, Give us of your oil; for our lamps are going out. But the wise answered, saying, Peradventure there will not be enough for us and you: go ye rather to them that sell, and buy for yourselves. And while they went away to buy, the bridegroom came; and they that were ready went in with him to the marriage feast: and the door was shut. Afterward came also the other virgins, saying, Lord, Lord, open to us. But he answered and said, Verily I say unto you, I know you not. Watch therefore, for ye know not the day nor the hour. (Matt. 25:1-13)

The verses in Matthew 24 regarding the Church concern the living believers. But what of those who will have died by the time of the Lord's coming? What will happen to them when Christ returns? The first parable in Matthew 25 speaks of them.

The Lord tells us of ten virgins, five of whom are wise and five foolish. Who are these virgins? Some believe the five wise virgins are genuine Christians, and the five foolish ones are unbelievers. However, although some of the virgins are wise and some are foolish, all of them are virgins. Where does the Scripture ever refer to the unbelievers as virgins before the Lord? How could an unbeliever ever be considered a virgin? To the contrary, Paul refers to the believers as virgins, saying,[1] *I espoused you to*

---
[1] 2 Cor. 11:2

one husband, that I might present you as a pure virgin to Christ. This indicates that all these virgins are believers.

Furthermore, the Lord does not say five of the virgins are wise and five are *false*. Rather, five are wise and five are *foolish*. They are all virgins but some are *foolish* virgins. Recall the apostle's word,[1] *O foolish Galatians, who did bewitch you.* It is indeed possible for the believers to be foolish. This also indicates that all the virgins are believers.

In addition, the foolish virgins call Jesus Lord, saying, *Lord, Lord, open to us.* How could any unbeliever call Jesus Lord? In truth, calling Jesus Lord makes you a believer.[2] This is a clear indication that the foolish virgins are Christians.

Moreover, all the virgins had oil in their lamps. Oil here indicates the Holy Spirit as the supply within the saints. Unbelievers have no oil whatsoever; otherwise they would be believers. All of these virgins could gain oil in their vessels as well, and eventually, all of them did. This again shows that all of them are believers. Not only are the wise virgins Christians, so also are the ones deemed foolish.

What then does this parable mean? The lamp of the virgins refers to their human spirit. In Proverbs, we are told that the spirit of man is the lamp of the Lord.[3] The vessels refer to their natural being, particularly their soul. The apostle Paul tells us that we have a treasure in earthen vessels.[4] The treasure is Christ, while the earthen vessel is our natural being.

All the virgins have oil in their lamps. This indicates that the Holy Spirit is within their human spirit.[5] In other words, they

---

[1] Gal. 3:1

[2] 1 Cor. 12:3

[3] Prov. 20:27

[4] 2 Cor. 4:7

[5] John 20:22; 3:6

have been regenerated, reborn. Indeed, he who is joined to the Lord is one spirit.[1]

The wise virgins brought oil with them in their vessels. This indicates that they had paid the necessary price to gain Christ as the Spirit in their souls. They had gained an extra supply of oil by how they had lived. This is to be sanctified and transformed. It is to have the Spirit of Christ spread within our hearts to impart what He is into our human being. This is to gain the oil.

The Lord says that all of these virgins slept. In other words, they all had died. When Stephen was martyred, he is termed to have fallen asleep.[2] And, in 1 Corinthians, Paul talks of the dead Christians as those who have fallen asleep.[3] In this parable, the Lord is telling us of all the Christians who will have died by the time of His return. In His view, they will have fallen asleep.

The Lord says that they all arose. Here, to arise from sleep means to be resurrected. Paul refers to this resurrection in both 1 Thessalonians[4] and 1 Corinthians.[5] At the last trumpet, all the Christians who have died and are awaiting the Lord's return will be resurrected.

When these virgins arise, they will all trim their wicks. This indicates that after resurrection there may still be a need to deal with certain matters. Even the wise virgins will have to trim their wicks, signifying that although they had gained an ample supply of oil during their lives, they will not yet have been fully perfected. Whether wise or foolish, all of these virgins will need to correct or adjust certain matters in their life or in their heart. Perhaps they will still have to repent for certain things said or done. Or, perhaps there will be certain character problems that remain. Whatever the case may be, all those resurrected at this time will have to deal with a kind of "burnt ash" that remains in their person. At that

---

[1] 1 Cor. 6:17

[2] Acts 7:60

[3] 1 Cor. 15:6, 18

[4] 1 Thes. 4:15-17

[5] 1 Cor. 15:51-52

time, there will be much repentance and many apologies among the Christians.

In resurrection, the real condition of every Christian will be manifested. Whether one has gained Christ as his supply or not will be seen by all. The Lord will shine forth brightly from those who have been wise to gain Him during their lives. But for those who have not—those who have been foolish, their great lack will become apparent. What they thought to be Christ will disappear in the reality of who and what Christ truly is. It will seem to them as if their lamps are going out. They had lived foolishly by not gaining Christ. Perhaps they had lived by following a religion and not the Spirit. Perhaps they had displayed a façade during their lives, a pretense of godliness, yet they had lived apart from Christ. At that moment, as Christ shines, their true inward emptiness and the falsehood of their living will be manifested. As their great lack is exposed, they will think their lamps are going out and ask the wise to give them some oil.

The wise will not share their supply of oil. How can they? They had gained this supply over many years of faithful service and contact with the Lord. They had paid the price during their lives to gain Christ.[1] That is, they had reckoned all things loss for the Lord. They had given up everything to gain Him. How could they share this? Rather, they tell the foolish ones to go to those who sell, and buy for themselves.

While the foolish go to buy the oil required to prepare them for the Lord, He will come as the wonderful bridegroom, and all those who are ready will go with Him into His feast. This is the thousand-year wedding feast during the millennial kingdom. It is the extraordinary joy in which so many of the Lord's believers will participate.

The crucial words here are, *all those who are ready*. It is not a matter of simply being a Christian. It is a matter of being a

---

[1] Phil. 3:8

Christian who is ready. To the living believers, the Lord commanded, *Be ready*.[1] To those who will have died, His command is the same: Be ready!

As those who are ready enter in with the Lord, the door will be shut behind them. The "list of invitees" to the wedding feast will be completed! The foolish, having spent the time necessary to buy oil—something they should have done during their lifetime by giving all for the Spirit—come back and cry out to the Lord from outside that closed door. This means that they must have gained the oil during the Millennium, while they were outside the glory of the wedding feast.

However, when they return, it is too late to enter. Their names had already been stricken from the guest list. And so the Lord says, *I know you not*. This is not to perish, not to be thrown into the lake of fire for eternity. It is to miss the enjoyment of the wedding feast during the thousand-year kingdom. Eventually, these foolish virgins will partake of the New Jerusalem. However, they will suffer a great loss during the Millennium by being outside the sweet and glorious enjoyment of Christ at His wedding feast.

The Apostle's Word

Look therefore carefully how ye walk, not as unwise, but as wise; redeeming the time, because the days are evil. Wherefore be ye not foolish, but understand what the will of the Lord is. And be not drunken with wine, wherein is riot, but be filled with the Spirit ... (Eph. 5:15-18)

In his epistle to the Ephesians, the Apostle Paul echoed the Lord's parable of the virgins. He told us to be wise and not be foolish. He charged us to walk carefully and redeem the time. This was his understanding of what the Lord meant when He said, *Watch!*

Furthermore, Paul tells us to be filled with the Spirit. This is the proper understanding of the Lord's word concerning the

---

[1] Matt. 24:44

virgins who took oil in their vessels. To take oil in one's vessel is to be filled with the Spirit, not only filled in one's human spirit—which all believers are—but also in one's soul.

In all this, what is the crucial point? Be ready! Pay the price now to obtain the oil. Watch. Pray. Open your heart to the Lord. Give Him the ground in your heart so that He might spread within you. Allow the Spirit within to move and flow. Speak Christ forth to others. Give of all that has been given to you. Trade. Trade to gain the oil. All of this corresponds to "watching" in Matthew 24. Whether we live or die, we must *watch* to be ready.

When the Lord comes for the believers, He will come from within. He will burst forth and in so doing all that we have become, whether good or bad, will be revealed. If we have been sanctified and transformed—inwardly filled with the Spirit—then we will enjoy the Lord's wonderful wedding feast. However, if we are not ready—not filled, but void of Christ—then we will suffer discipline for 1000 years.

A Hidden Warning

There is a serious warning hidden in plain sight within the parable of the 10 virgins. Consider: who are those who sell? If they can sell oil, they must have an abundant supply of it. That is, they must be full of the Spirit. However, these are outside the wedding feast for the duration of the Millennium. How can this be?

These are not particular, named people. Rather, these are those who for some reason are not given entry to the kingdom, despite the abundant supply they have. They were given a particular and great portion of the Spirit to supply and impart to others. But for some reason, they will be denied entry into the kingdom. Perhaps they had a grave issue with pride or some other significant problem. Consider Moses: although he spent 40 years leading the children of Israel through the wilderness, he was not allowed to enter the good land.[1] He had a serious issue that cost

---

[1] Num. 27:12-14

him dearly. So it will be with some who have been endowed with a great supply of the Spirit.

Yes, some may have a considerable supply of the Spirit, so much so that they can actually "sell" it to others. But, be warned and be humbled. Do not think highly of yourself. You can still be outside the kingdom despite this great supply; you can experience something akin to what Moses did.

This is the second serious warning to those who have been granted an abundant supply. Whether they have been given food to feed or oil to supply God's people, the Lord warns of serious consequences for those who misuse what they have been given and mistreat the believers. *They will miss the wedding feast!*

The Talents

For it is as when a man, going into another country, called his own servants, and delivered unto them his goods. And unto one he gave five talents, to another two, to another one; to each according to his several ability; and he went on his journey. Straightway he that received the five talents went and traded with them, and made other five talents. In like manner he also that received the two gained other two. But he that received the one went away and digged in the earth, and hid his lord's money. Now after a long time the lord of those servants cometh, and maketh a reckoning with them. And he that received the five talents came and brought other five talents, saying, Lord, thou deliveredst unto me five talents: lo, I have gained other five talents. His lord said unto him, Well done, good and faithful servant: thou hast been faithful over a few things, I will set thee over many things; enter thou into the joy of thy lord. And he also that received the two talents came and said, Lord, thou deliveredst unto me two talents: lo, I have gained other two talents. His lord said unto him, Well done, good and faithful servant: thou hast been faithful over a few things, I will set thee over many things; enter thou into the joy of thy lord. And he also that had received the one talent came and said, Lord, I knew thee that thou art a hard man, reaping where thou didst not sow, and gathering where thou didst not scatter; and I was afraid, and went away and hid thy talent in the earth: lo, thou hast thine own. But his lord answered and said unto him, Thou wicked and slothful servant, thou knewest that I reap where I sowed not, and gather where I did not scatter; thou oughtest therefore to have put my money to the bankers, and at my coming I should have received back mine own with interest. Take ye away therefore the talent from him, and give it unto him that hath the ten talents. For unto every one that hath shall be given, and he shall have abundance: but from him that hath not, even that which he hath shall be taken away. And cast ye out the unprofitable servant into the outer darkness: there shall be the weeping and the gnashing of teeth. (Matt. 25:14-30)

Following the parable of the virgins is the parable of the talents. This is a general word spoken to both the living and dead believers. It is not in any way connected to the unbelievers. The unbelievers are not the Lord's servants, nor are they given any kind of spiritual gift. It is the believers who are given gifts of grace from the Spirit.[1] Some may receive a single gift from the Spirit, while others may receive multiple gifts. But either way, it is the believers who receive the Lord's "talents."

The crucial point in this parable is not whether we have a talent. That is, it is not whether we are a Christian or not. All those in this parable have at least one talent. In other words, all are Christians. What is crucial here is what we do with the talent we have been given, what we do with the spiritual gift we have received from God. Do we invest it or hide it?

Those who invest what the Lord has given them gain more. The gift of the Spirit multiplies by use. It multiplies by "trading" it with others. As we impart what we have been given to others, what we have received grows and multiplies. Not only are others enriched, but we ourselves are as well.

In addition, as we impart what we have to others, we also receive from them. What we receive becomes ours. We are also enriched in this way. We gain by giving and we gain by receiving. It is this kind of "trade," this kind of "investment," that produces an increase in the gift of grace we have been given.

---

[1] 1 Pet. 4:10; Eph. 4:7

On the other hand, those who hide their talent gain nothing more. Our talent does not increase unless it is used. Burying within ourselves what the Lord has given, guarantees that it will *not* grow, that it will *not* multiply.

What is the one who hides his talent doing during his life? In other words, if this one is not spending his time in a spiritually profitable way, then how is his time being spent? The one who is hiding the talent must be in the world, in the flesh, in the self. This one must be apart from Christ and spending time elsewhere. We all must be doing something. If we are not spending our time wisely to invest what the Lord has given us, then we must be spending it elsewhere, apart from Christ. Therefore, the Lord calls the one who hides his talent *wicked and slothful.*

Interestingly, there is no case mentioned of one who invests his talent and loses it. This is because this cannot happen! In every case, when we invest our spiritual gift, we gain. It is simply not possible to lose it. We either invest and gain, or hide and do not gain.

There is something more in this parable: the Lord indicates by His choice of examples that those servants of His who have received multiple talents—multiple gifts—invest. It is those who have been endowed with but a single talent who hide it. This does not mean that every single-talented believer hides their gift. Rather, it indicates that the problem of hiding one's spiritual gift is mostly with those who have a single talent.

The Judgment Seat

For we must all be made manifest before the judgment-seat of Christ; that each one may receive the things done in the body, according to what he hath done, whether it be good or bad. (2 Cor. 5:10)

Paul tells us that we will all stand before the judgment seat of Christ and give account for the things we have done in our bodies, whether good or bad. This will happen when all the believers are gathered to the Lord in the air at the sounding of the seventh trumpet. These include the Christians remaining on Earth at that time, as well as the ones who are resurrected.

At His coming, the Lord will first judge all the believers at His judgment seat. Those who spent their time on Earth investing what the Lord had given them will be highly rewarded. They will enter into the joy of the Lord and feast with Him 1000 years. In addition, they will be assigned rule over cities,[1] over many things,[2] even over all that He has,[3] including things such as the forces of nature. This will be the most excellent time. Every believer should hunger for this, and long to gain in this age all that is necessary to be prepared for the next.

On the other hand, there will be those who have hidden their talent. These too will answer to the Lord for what they did while on the Earth. The Lord calls these not simply foolish, but evil. This indicates that they have spent their time doing evil things. It also indicates that apart from Christ and from using our spiritual gift, what we do is evil. This is a serious and sobering word. If we do not invest our talent by using the spiritual gift we have been given, then the Lord sees us as evil and performing evil.

The ones who hide their talent are cast into outer darkness. This is to be outside the joy of the kingdom and outside the brilliance of Christ's glory. They will continue in the darkness of their previous life apart from Christ—and continue there until the spiritual gift they have been given has fully grown and is fully exercised. In that outer darkness, there will be weeping in repentance for slothfulness in the previous earthly life and gnashing of teeth at missing the thousand years of the wedding feast. This will indeed be a woeful state.

Watchfulness in this age and wisdom in gaining an extra supply of the oil of the Spirit speak of the divine life and its growth within us. Investing the talents speaks of our service for and before the Lord. These go hand-in-hand. If we are watchful and wise, then we are investing. If we are slothful or sleeping, then we are

---

[1] Luke 19:16-17

[2] Matt. 25:21, 23

[3] Matt. 24:46

hiding our talent. May we all receive with a sober mind the warnings given to us by the Lord in these verses.

CHAPTER 4

The Nations

But when the Son of man shall come in his glory, and all the angels with him, then shall he sit on the throne of his glory: and before him shall be gathered all the nations: and he shall separate them one from another, as the shepherd separateth the sheep from the goats; and he shall set the sheep on his right hand, but the goats on the left. Then shall the King say unto them on his right hand, Come, ye blessed of my Father, inherit the kingdom prepared for you from the foundation of the world: for I was hungry, and ye gave me to eat; I was thirsty, and ye gave me drink; I was a stranger, and ye took me in; naked, and ye clothed me; I was sick, and ye visited me; I was in prison, and ye came unto me. Then shall the righteous answer him, saying, Lord, when saw we thee hungry, and fed thee? or athirst, and gave thee drink? And when saw we thee a stranger, and took thee in? or naked, and clothed thee? And when saw we thee sick, or in prison, and came unto thee? And the King shall answer and say unto them, Verily I say unto you, Inasmuch as ye did it unto one of these my brethren, even these least, ye did it unto me. Then shall he say also unto them on the left hand, Depart from me, ye cursed, into the eternal fire which is prepared for the devil and his angels: for I was hungry, and ye did not give me to eat; I was thirsty, and ye gave me no drink; I was a stranger, and ye took me not in; naked, and ye clothed me not; sick, and in prison, and ye visited me not. Then shall they also answer, saying, Lord, when saw we thee hungry, or athirst, or a stranger, or naked, or sick, or in prison, and did not minister unto thee? Then shall he answer them, saying, Verily I say unto you, Inasmuch as ye did it not unto one of these least, ye did it not unto me. And these shall go away into eternal punishment: but the righteous into eternal life. (Matt. 25:31-46)

The final section of verses in Matthew 25 speaks of the third of the three peoples on Earth—the nations. The nations are all the people on Earth who are neither Christians nor Jews. In this section, the Lord speaks in clear words. This portion corresponds to the parable about the fish in Matthew 13.[1] In both of these, the Lord is speaking of the nations.

The sign of the Lord's presence to the nations is His physical appearing and His sitting upon His throne of glory in judgment. The nations will not know nor understand about the Lord's presence until He is physically among them. At least some of them will fear God and be aware of His judgment upon the Earth. But they will not understand that He, as the Son of God who became the man Jesus, is about to appear.

At the very end of the age, after the Lord has slaughtered all the armies invading Israel, He will send forth his angels to gather all the remaining people on Earth. These will include any Jews who have been scattered during their great tribulation and any of the people of the Earth who remain alive. All the nations will be gathered to the valley of Jehoshaphat[2] in Israel. There will be no place to hide from the angels, nor can any doors bar them from entering. Whether in the heart of a mountain or in the depth of a deep underground shelter, there will be no place to hide. The searching eyes of the Lord's angels will find every human being on Earth and bring them to the valley of Jehoshaphat for judgment.

There the angels will separate the nations into two groups: the sheep who will stand on the Lord's right hand, and the goats who will be at His left. They will all be judged there by the Lord according to how they have treated the Lord's brothers—both His physical brothers, the Jews, and His spiritual brothers, the believers. It will be according to how they treated the Lord's brothers *during the endtime*, for it is then that human suffering will be at its peak.

Some among the nations—those who will be at His right hand—will have shown the Lord's brothers proper and compassionate care. They will have clothed those who were naked, fed those who were hungry, gave a drink to those who were thirsty,

---

[1] Matt. 13:47-50

[2] Joel 3:2-3

visited those who were in prison or were sick. Such a caring heart for the Lord's people in the midst of such great opposition will be much blessed by the Lord and by God. These "sheep" will enter into the glory of the thousand-year kingdom to become the nations there and to repopulate the Earth. They will enter into eternal life. Eternal life is not only the divine life shared and enjoyed by the believers. It is also a realm into which the blessed of the nations will enter. It is the realm of the divine life manifested through Christ and the many sons of God. Those who enter into that realm will never die.

On the Lord's left hand will be gathered those of the nations who have treated His brothers improperly. When His brothers were hungry, thirsty, naked, sick, alone, or in prison, these did not come to their aid. This shows that they not only lacked care and compassion for God's people, but that they were filled with hatred toward the Jews and the believers. They hated the Jews and the believers because these belonged to Christ, and they hated Christ. They hated Christ because God is in Christ, and they hated God. Their hatred towards the Lord's brothers had at its very heart a hatred of God Himself. As a consequence, they will be cast into eternal fire, the fire which has been prepared for the devil and his angels. Satan and those of the angels who have followed him will partake of this fire at the end of the thousand-year kingdom. However, since these goats followed Satan by mistreating God's people, they will be cast into that fire for eternal punishment, sharing Satan's fate.

This will be a time of great decision. The eternal destiny of many will be decided as the Lord sits upon His throne of glory. To some it will be eternal relief, joy, and blessing. To others, it will be eternal anguish and suffering: they will not be able to escape the brilliant and burning glory of the holy and righteous God.

CHAPTER 5

A Further Word

Then shall two men be in the field; one is taken, and one is left: two women shall be grinding at the mill; one is taken, and one is left. (Matt. 24:40-41)

Matthew 24 and 25 are truly marvelous chapters. In these, the Lord not only tells us what will transpire from the time of His death until the end of the age, He also speaks to each of the three peoples on Earth. He reveals the various conditions of the believers at the end of the age, and additionally speaks of both Israel and the nations. He sums up the endtime in two chapters! This is simply marvelous.

We have examined the crucial parts of Matthew 24-25 in some depth in the previous chapters of this book. As is typically the case with the word of God, there is still more. Hidden within these words in Matthew is something completely unexpected, which opens the door to a whole new world of sorts.

Let us examine Matthew 24:40-41. It is these two verses that were before my eyes when I was awakened in the middle of the night. What was it that stood out? By what was I puzzled? It was the Lord's use of the definite article in both these verses. He said two men will be in *the* field; two women will be grinding at *the* mill. Why did He use *the*? Why not *a* field and *a* mill.[1] Why did he select the definite article in both these cases?

The Lord is precise in His speaking. He never wastes words, He never adds words unnecessarily, and He never speaks casually. So then why did He use the definite article? For example, He could

---

[1] In Greek, there is a definite article, but no indefinite one. The indefinite article is indicated by the lack of the definite article. In this case, the definite article is present with both *field* and *mill*.

have said *some* fields. But He chose to use the definite article. He did this knowingly and purposefully. As I looked into this, one question after another came to mind. It was like finding a hidden door which opened to another realm or dimension. It was as if a whole book had been hidden in the simple word *the*.

A Specific Word

I had always thought these verses were a kind of general word—the Lord was referring to some non-specific place or places on Earth where these kinds of events would take place. But His use of the word *the* indicates otherwise. This is not something nonspecific. The Lord must have been viewing a particular scene in the future and using that scene as representative of all the Christians on Earth at that time. It seems obvious to me now that the Lord used the definite article to point us to that particular scene He was viewing because of its importance. And I, like so many others, simply never noticed those peculiar definite articles. Then what scene was He viewing?

Furthermore, the word *the* indicates something that is in some way singular. The Lord certainly was not meaning that there will only be one field and one mill on the entire Earth. That seems obvious. What then was He viewing? In the scene He was looking at, there was only one field and one mill—the field and the mill in that locale He saw. But again, what locale? And, why did the Lord use this locale as an example?

The Early Church

I am reminded of the early church. There the believers had all things common.[1] They were enjoying a kind of divine "community," one that was ruled by God and not by a set of communal regulations. This continued until the Hebrew believers began mistreating the widows among the Grecian Jews, neglecting them in their daily ministration of food.[2] This in turn resulted in

---

[1] Acts 2:44-45

[2] Acts 6:1

murmuring among the Grecian Jews. That ended the divine "community" among them. It has evidently never been recovered.

This was lost due to the lack of Christ among the believers of the early church. They all were quite young in the Lord and had not experienced Christ sufficiently: their selves were still quite active and not on the cross; apparently, their flesh was quite active as well. Simply put, they were immature in the divine life. As the joy, exuberance, and anticipation of their initial salvation waned, the inward condition of the believers was exposed. This is similar to the water in a river dissipating and exposing the rocks beneath the surface.

I believe the Lord must have been viewing some practicing the proper church life, something that will come into being sometime in the future near the end of the age. Indeed, it might be the appearance, finally, of a proper church life that moves God to end the age. Such a church life will be maintained by mature believers, to whom Christ is everything. To these believers, possessions are for all. They are living in God and are one in Him. As the Lord said in His prayer to the Father, all things that are Mine are Yours, and Yours are Mine.[1] After thousands of years, the proper church life will finally be recovered. However, this will not come about due to some kind of agreement among the believers to share all things. That would simply be another kind of human commune. This will come about through the experience of the believers as they live in God, where all things *are* common.

In this context, there is *only* one field and one mill. Evidently, all things are common there. And this gives rise to various other questions:

Why did the Lord say the *field* (singular) and not the *fields* (plural)?

Why are the men in the field and the women at the mill? In other words, why are the men and women separated, at least to some degree?

---
[1] John 17:10

Why did the Lord select the field and the mill for His examples?

Why were the women grinding? In our current world, is not all grinding of grain automated?

Why does it not mention what the men were doing in the field? The women were grinding; what were the men doing?

Why *two* men and *two* women?

Here the Lord said two men shall be in the field. He did not say they will be in the *fields*, like He did when speaking of the prodigal son.[1] Instead, He chose the singular form of *field*. Why? This should indicate that the gathering of believers which He was viewing was small. There was one field for all of them. Indeed, the Lord does not want a great megachurch. That which is great is not according to God's heart.

In Matthew 13 the Lord speaks of the mustard seed that becomes a tree. The mutation of that little herb into a tree is abhorrent to God. What the Lord desires is something small and spreading. He is the vine; we are the branches. He does not want the vine to become a great tree; rather, He wants the vine to spread throughout the Earth as a vine. So here, when the Lord is viewing the proper church life, His words indicate that the gathering of the believers there was small.

The town of Bethany is an example of what the Lord desires for the Church. It was small and unobtrusive. While the Lord spent time regularly in Jerusalem, speaking God's word for the salvation of any Jews whose hearts were open, He ate in Bethany[2] and spent His nights there.[3]

The church in Philadelphia is another example of what is on the Lord's heart. Philadelphia had but a little strength.[4] She was

---

[1] Luke 15:15

[2] Mark 14:3

[3] Matt. 21:17

[4] Rev. 3:7-8

despised by those who considered themselves God's people.[1] But Philadelphia was and is loved by the Lord. It is not greatness that the Lord desires. Rather, it is lowliness, meekness, reality, and much love.

The Lord speaks of the men being in the field and the women being at the mill. Why this separation? Here the Lord is showing the proper separation in the church. The men being in the field and the women working at the mill helps to limit the indulgence of the flesh. It keeps sin at bay by not providing an opportunity for it. This shows a wise and healthy respect for man's true condition while in the flesh, and indicates a proper church life in the midst of our grossly sinful world.

The field and the mill are cited together by the Lord in these verses as one more indication that He was looking at a particular scene. What grows in the field is ground at the mill. These two go hand-in-hand. Furthermore, the ones in the field and at the mill are laboring to provide for the necessities of life. They are one in their labor. They are working together to produce and provide food. By mentioning these two together, the Lord was pointing us to that very scene He was viewing.

The women are grinding at the mill. However, in our current day, virtually all grinding of grain is automated. Why then would the women be grinding at the mill? Perhaps they choose to do so out of the desire for simplicity. Alternatively, they may be forced to do so by the world situation at that time. Perhaps certain disasters will have rendered the use of automation impossible. Whatever the case may be, the women are tasked with the somewhat strenuous work of grinding grain.

The Lord says the women are grinding at the mill. But the men are simply *in the field*. Why did the Lord not mention what they were doing? It must be that the men will have finished their work at that time. That is, they will have finished harvesting the whole field. Indeed, that is why the women are grinding: the men have harvested. This tells us something about the time of the year when the Lord will return for His believers.

---

[1] Rev. 3:9

Finally, the Lord could have chosen many scenes from which believers will be taken as His example. He selected this one, where there are *two* men in the field and *two* women at the mill. Why two? Aside from the Lord describing the actual scene He was viewing, He was telling us that in that day, there will be only two alternatives for Christians: we will either be taken or left. There is no other possibility.

In this short passage, the Lord gives us a picture of the endtime church life being practiced and enjoyed. It is this He has desired from the beginning: the oneness of the three-one God—the Triune God or Trinity—being lived out through the believers as they live together with one another. How beautiful that scene is! Additionally, this proper church life will be an example and template for those who are left behind during the last years of this age. This practice of the proper church life will be a blueprint for all those believers to follow as they live together and struggle through the few last years of this age.

During that time, due to the enormous upheavals striking the Earth and the great hardships proceeding from them, the believers still on Earth will have no choice but to share all things and live peaceably together in order to survive. While such intense suffering is not what God wants for the believers, He has nevertheless provided an alternative way to help them into His heart's desire.

Yet Another Warning

... one is left ... (Matt. 24:40)

It seems difficult to understand how any of those who have entered into the proper church practice, let go of their personal possessions, and lived in oneness with the believers could be left behind. But in this example is another great warning. It is not enough to follow an outward practice. We must have the inward reality that is Christ Himself within us. We must be able to say, as the apostle did: *It is no longer I that live, but Christ lives in me*,[1] and *For me to live is Christ*.[2] It is only this that prepares us for the Lord's return.

In that day, there will likely be some who enter into the practice of the proper church life because of its social aspects. These believers find the social relationships in the church life extremely appealing. Others may be attracted by the beauty of that church life. But they may be sorely lacking in their person-to-person relationship with Christ. Still others may enter into this practice because they believe it to be a kind of new movement, something which they find enticing. Whatever the case, may we all be warned. May we all be sober-minded and serious. There is only one thing that will qualify us to be taken in that day: gaining Christ by being watchful and prayerful. As we do so, the Lord may very well lead us into this proper church life of which we have spoken. But, practicing that church life does not necessarily mean we have gained Christ for our entry into His kingdom.

---

[1] Gal. 2:20

[2] Phil. 1:21

CHAPTER 6

A Pleased God

But why did the Lord choose this particular scene—two in the field and two grinding at the mill—when He spoke of His secret coming? The answer to this question requires some explanation.

God's Desire

Blessed be the God and Father of our Lord Jesus Christ, who hath blessed us with every spiritual blessing in the heavenly places in Christ: even as he chose us in him before the foundation of the world, that we should be holy and without blemish before him in love: having foreordained us unto adoption as sons through Jesus Christ unto himself, according to the good pleasure of his will, to the praise of the glory of his grace, which he freely bestowed on us in the Beloved ... (Eph. 1:3-6)

Unto me, who am less than the least of all saints, was this grace given, to preach unto the Gentiles the unsearchable riches of Christ; and to make all men see what is the dispensation of the mystery which for ages hath been hid in God who created all things; to the intent that now unto the principalities and the powers in the heavenly places might be made known through the church the manifold wisdom of God, according to the eternal purpose which he purposed in Christ Jesus our Lord... (Eph. 3:8-11)

Before God created anything, in eternity past, God had a deep desire—something for which His heart longed. This desire is His eternal purpose.[1] This purpose has many aspects. In one way,

---

[1] Eph. 3:9-11

it is many sons for Him. In another, it is a bride[1] for Christ. In still another, it is a spiritual house[2], a temple,[3] and a city,[4] in which He would dwell.

God desires His many sons to be like Him in every way (except that they would not share His Godhead[5]). They are to share His attributes[6]—His kindness, gentleness, long-suffering, lowliness, righteousness, faithfulness, holiness, and perhaps countless others.

They are also to share His divine life,[7] making Him truly their Father[8] and them His genuine sons.[9] They are to share His divine nature.[10] They are even to share His own glory.[11] He desires sons befitting the Being that He is.

These many sons are even to share His position,[12] His status, His station. They are to be exalted, because they share His lowly

---

[1] Eph. 5:31-32; Rev. 19:7-8

[2] 1 Pet. 2:5

[3] Eph. 2:19-22

[4] Rev. 21:2-3

[5] The Godhead is what makes God God. God is God by virtue of who and what He is. We share in all He is by virtue of who *He* is, not by virtue of who *we* are. That is, we share His many attributes and His position by Christ being in us and by us being in Christ. This is not something of ourselves, but of God. While God is God because of who He is, we become Him not because of ourselves, but because of who He is in and to us. Consequently, we do not and can not share His Godhead.

[6] 1 Pet. 2:9; 2 Pet. 2:3

[7] John 3:36; Eph. 4:18

[8] John 20:17

[9] John 1:12-13

[10] 2 Pet. 2:4

[11] John 17:22

[12] Eph. 1:4; 2:6

and meek nature.[1] They are to rule over His creation,[2] because they are to be righteous,[3] just as He is righteous. They can be entrusted with many responsibilities because they are to be faithful,[4] just as He is faithful.

Furthermore, they are to share God's oneness.[5] God is three, yet God is one. How is God one? In every way. God is one in character, thought, purpose, desire. He is one in every way, and yet the Three of the Godhead—Father, Son, and Spirit—are distinct. God's sons are to share this oneness. They are to be one in His life,[6] in His nature,[7] and in His expression.[8] There are to think the same thing[9] and be one in spirit and soul.[10] Briefly, they are to be one in God, as God Himself is one. This is God's eternal desire.

God's Working

I pray for them: I pray not for the world, but for those whom thou hast given me; for they are thine: and all things that are mine are thine, and thine are mine: and I am glorified in them. And I am no more in the world, and these are in the world, and I come to thee. Holy Father, keep them in thy name which thou hast given me, that they may be one, even as we are. (Jn. 17:9-11)

Sanctify them in the truth: thy word is truth. As thou didst send me into the world, even so sent I them into the world. And for their sakes I sanctify myself, that they themselves also may be sanctified

---

[1] Matt. 11:29

[2] Matt. 5:5

[3] Matt. 13:43

[4] Matt. 25:21, 23

[5] John 17:11

[6] John 17:11

[7] John 17:17, 21

[8] John 17:22

[9] Phil. 2:2

[10] Phil. 1:27

in truth. Neither for these only do I pray, but for them also that believe on me through their word; that they may all be one; even as thou, Father, art in me, and I in thee, that they also may be in us: that the world may believe that thou didst send me.   (Jn. 17:17-21)

And the glory which thou hast given me I have given unto them; that they may be one, even as we are one; I in them, and thou in me, that they may be perfected into one; that the world may know that thou didst send me, and lovedst them, even as thou lovedst me. (Jn. 17:22-23)

God has worked towards the goal of His eternal purpose step-by-step for billions of years, since even before the creation. He has never lost sight of His goal, nor can He be deterred. Even His adversary, Satan, with all the fallen angels, cannot stop God from obtaining His heart's desire.

For His purpose, God became a man—the man named Jesus. And, for this purpose, Jesus died on the cross and rose again. Shortly before His death, He prayed that all those who believe into Him would be one in the divine life, the divine nature, and the divine glory.

He asked God the Father to keep all the believers in the Father's name.[1] The name "Father" indicates that He is the source of life. To keep the believers in His name is to keep them in and by the divine life. The believers are one in life: that is, they all share the same divine life of their divine Father. They have been born of the Father, and partake of and enjoy His divine life. This is the first aspect of the oneness of the believers.

Next, he prayed to the Father to sanctify the believers in the truth. Sanctification means to make holy. God makes the believers holy by imparting His own holy element into them. He imparts His divine element and divine substance. This changes the nature of the believers and makes them holy within, holy in reality. Being made holy in such a way is eternal. It can never be undone. This is the second aspect of the believers' oneness. It is to be one in the divine nature which has been imparted into them.

---

[1] John 17:11

Finally, Jesus prayed for them to be one in the divine glory, which He has given to the believers. This is to be one in expression. Glory is God expressed in His splendor. The believers are to be one in their expression of the divine Person. This is the perfecting of their character. In various ways, through each of the believers, the divine Person is to be expressed. These are the marvelous sons of God being one in God Himself.

A Window

This prayer of the Lord provides a window into the divine Being. The Lord says that all that is the Father's is His, and all that is His is the Father's. Everything is shared between them. Nothing is withheld. How tender and heart-touching this is. How great is the love between the Father and the Son in the divine Trinity. How precious and pleasant is Their relationship and state of being.

However, consider our fallen condition. Within us are animosity, greed, contention, envy, pride, lust, stubbornness, hardheartedness, religion, self-righteousness, self-defense, and so very many other negative elements. There is no place for any of these in God. These must be eliminated forever. Furthermore, deeply ingrained into us is our sense of possession, of personal wealth and ownership. This simply does not exist in God. As we enter into God, all of this is removed. We are left in the exquisite state of oneness that God is.

As the divine life with the divine nature works within us, all the negative elements are removed bit by bit. The temporary negative evils within us are replaced by the eternal divine attributes. God's great love for us is imparted into us, producing within us a great love toward God, toward the Lord Jesus, toward the believers, and eventually toward all men and even the whole creation. This is God's heart being reproduced in His many sons. With such a love, we give and share freely. We give freely to our children; we should give and share even more with our eternal, divine family.

God Satisfied

It is only by this that we can arrive at full-grown sons of God.[1] Living together in such a state is the real and proper church life. This is something God has longed for, Christ has prayed for, and for which He has poured out everything. Recall the parable of the merchant and the pearls.[2] When the merchant found a pearl of great price, he sold all that he had and bought it. The pearl of great price is the Church. Christ sold all that He had for her!

In this proper church life, there is a sweet harmony, like the sweetest of symphonies. There is nothing existing that compares with the oneness of God. His great desire is to bring all of His sons into that wonderful state of being. When this comes into existence on the Earth, it will capture God's heart, even as His desire for this has already captured His heart. This is what He has longed for and desired from eternity past. And, it is those who have reached this goal that the Lord will take in that day.

So then, why was the Lord viewing this scene in Matthew 24? It is because His eyes have always been on this scene, even from eternity past. From the beginning until now He sees this, a proper living of the believers in the oneness of God. In fact, He cannot take His eyes off this.

In His resurrection, Christ is called the Firstborn among many brothers.[3] He is the first man to be designated a son of God in resurrection.[4] Many brothers will follow. In the scene Christ is viewing, He is looking at the first of His many brothers being born! These are the first men to follow in the Lord's footsteps to become sons of God in every way. Finally, after billions of years, countless arrangements, innumerable interventions, workings of many sorts, God's heart is satisfied. What He longs for comes into existence at that time when those who are taken appear before His

---

[1] Eph. 4:13

[2] Matt. 13:45-46

[3] Rom. 8:29; Rev. 1:5

[4] Rom. 1:4

throne in celebration of all that He has done. How pleasing this is to our Father!

CHAPTER 7

One

What is oneness? What is being one? To understand this, it is helpful first to see what oneness is not.

Not Conformity

Oneness is *not* the practice of conformity, although many have believed that it was. Oneness is not a matter of wearing the same clothes, nor is it a matter of having the same kind of electronics. It is not exhibiting the same kind of behavior. Agreeing with something because others do is also not oneness. This is often nothing more than sycophancy. Under the surface of sycophantic behavior is darkness.

Some Christian leaders pressure others to go along with their way. They call this oneness. This is false. This is not according to truth, and is actually against the truth.

Oneness is not any kind of outward practice. It is not a practice of being outwardly the same in any way. Outward-conforming practice stems from the human mind attempting to generate oneness. However, this actually hinders God substantially. Oneness cannot be generated by man, and is not of man.

Not a Human Leader

Following what a human leader says and does because he is the leader is also not oneness. Agreeing with such a leader—regardless of whether he practices good or evil—is not only not being one, it is something indicative of a cult. We follow others according to how they follow Christ. If they are not following Christ, we must not follow them.

Not a Set of Doctrines

Subscribing to a set of doctrines is also not oneness. Each Christian denomination has a set of doctrines. Following these doctrines makes one a member of that denomination. However, that is not oneness. To be a member of a denomination is to denominate yourself. That is to call yourself by some name other than Christ. By doing this, you are actually dividing yourself from others. This is the opposite of oneness.

Not of Human Origin

Not only is oneness not of human origin, it cannot be. It is not men attempting to be one in any way. It is not compromising or reaching a settlement. These are not oneness. Oneness is not manufactured; it is not of human doing. In fact, it is not humanly possible to be one. *Everything* in the human realm is not oneness.

God Himself

Believest thou not that I am in the Father, and the Father in me? the words that I say unto you I speak not from myself: but the Father abiding in me doeth his works. Believe me that I am in the Father, and the Father in me: or else believe me for the very works' sake. (Jn. 14:10-11)

What is oneness? Oneness is God Himself. Oneness is a divine attribute of God. Outside of God, there is no oneness. Oneness is the divine Trinity, dwelling One in the Other—coinhering. The Three of the Godhead—Father, Son, and Spirit—are inseparable, yet They are distinct. The Father is in the Son and the Son is in the Father; the Son became the Spirit,[1] and the Spirit is the eyes of the Son.[2] God is Spirit.[3] Therefore, the Father and the Son, who are both God, are also Spirit. This Spirit must be the

---

[1] 1 Cor. 15:45

[2] Rev. 5:6

[3] John 4:24

Holy Spirit; otherwise there would be two divine Spirits. The Son is even called the Father.[1] This may all sound confusing, but God is not for our mind's understanding. God is for us to experience. The Father comes to us in the Son through the Spirit, and by experiencing that indwelling Spirit, we experience the Son and the Father as well.

By being three and yet one, God manifests something about Himself—something about how He is—that would otherwise not be known. By being three and yet one, God makes known His oneness, His being one. This attribute of oneness comes forth from God being love. Just as God's attributes of kindness, compassion, gentleness, and so many others stem from God being love, so does God being one.

Because God is love, many things cannot exist in God: envy, jealousy, contention, strife, and various other evils. How can any of these exist in God, if the three are one? They simply cannot. And so, since the three are truly one, the Lord says in His prayer, all that is Yours is Mine, and all that is Mine is Yours.[2]

God's Working

For whom he foreknew, he also foreordained to be conformed to the image of his Son, that he might be the firstborn among many brethren ... (Rom 8:29)

Blessed be the God and Father of our Lord Jesus Christ, who according to his great mercy begat us again unto a living hope by the resurrection of Jesus Christ from the dead ... (1 Pet. 1:3)

It appears, then, that God has done everything, and this is *almost* true. God created[3] all things, including us. He became a man[4]—Jesus—and manifested God to the whole creation. In

---

[1] Isa. 9:6

[2] John 17:10

[3] Gen. 1:1; Heb. 1:2

[4] John 1:14

everything this man did, God was seen. Jesus' human virtues displayed the divine attributes. His compassion, kindness, love, discernment, and His many other virtues revealed God.

Jesus died on the cross.[1] He did so willingly.[2] By doing this, He atoned for sins.[3] He also condemned sin in the flesh.[4] Furthermore, He tasted death for everything.[5] He did not taste of death for man only—He tasted death on behalf of *every thing*. Through His death, He destroyed the devil.[6] He also crucified the old man.[7] And of great importance, He released the divine life from within Himself,[8] so that man could partake of this life.

He rose again, and in so doing conquered death.[9] In His resurrection, He begot us all to a living hope and became the Firstborn among many brothers. He was once God's only begotten Son, but in His resurrection in His humanity, He became the Firstborn. He was the first of many brothers—the many sons of God. After His resurrection, He breathed the Spirit[10] as life into His disciples. This is something every Christian enjoys—that divine life!

He then ascended to the highest possible place, to the very throne of God.[11] God made Him Lord[12] of all. He is ruling everything.

---

[1] John 19:17-18, 30

[2] John 10:17-18

[3] 1 Cor. 15:3; 1 John 2:2

[4] Rom. 8:3

[5] Heb. 2:9

[6] Heb. 2:14

[7] Rom. 6:6

[8] John 12:24

[9] Rev. 1:18

[10] John 20:22

[11] Eph. 4:10; Rev. 3:21

[12] Acts 2:36

Finally, the Spirit was poured out upon the believers,[1] thereby enabling them to experience and enjoy the mystical body[2] of Christ.

Our Part

What then is left to be done? There is one thing that remains: our inward being. Despite all God has done, He cannot touch us inwardly without our permission. He has given us a free will, and He respects that free will to the utmost. He needs our cooperation to apply all that He has done outwardly to us inwardly. In all of God's plan and in all that He has done to accomplish that plan, the most crucial item is our cooperation. It is by our cooperation, or lack thereof, that God's plan either proceeds or is frustrated.

Despite all God has done, inwardly we may have been barely touched. Our inward condition may be virtually the same as it was five or even ten years ago. We may have been very busy doing many things outwardly, yet inwardly we are stagnating or—even worse—some inward infection has been festering. What God requires is our cooperation.

We must cooperate with the shining and searching Spirit. We must allow this Spirit everywhere within us. If we do so, the Spirit will expose the hidden things within our heart. He will illuminate what is within and thereby put to death everything that is not of God.

We must cooperate with the divine life, which was imparted into us when we were reborn. We must nourish that life with God's word and with prayer. We must allow that life to grow and spread within us.

We must pray more, *much more*. There is so much need for prayer. There is need to pray not only for so many outward circumstances and developments upon the Earth, but we ourselves have a great need for prayer. We must give the Lord the ground in

---

[1] Acts 2:33

[2] 1 Cor. 12:13

our hearts and repent for so many hidden evils, attitudes, desires, and perceptions. We do not need to *do*; we need to *pray*.

Prayer should not be a formality. Rather, we must touch God in our prayer, and pray what is in God's heart. We must commune with God, fellowship with Him, and have a conversation with Him. This is real prayer. We may also feel the need to fast as well, as a means to deny the flesh.

We must give everything—absolutely everything—to the Lord. If we are serious with Him, we will withhold nothing. We give not only those things that are outward; we give our heart and every part of it. We give until we are empty of everything, and ready for Him to fill.

Layers

We all have many "layers" within us. These are layers of problems, which have been built up over the years, one layer after another. Rather than deal with them as they occur, we ignore them. And so, they accumulate one upon another. The more they accumulate, the more difficult it is to free ourselves from them. They require our immediate and focused attention before the Lord. Layer by layer, we must bring each to the Lord in prayer. We pray over each one until it disappears, and the Lord moves on to the next.

We must continue this kind of prayer layer by layer, deeper and deeper, unraveling the Gordian knot that is our heart, until our very core is reached. It is likely we have buried what is deep inside us under many layers because of fear. But, do not run and hide from what is deep within. With the Lord, there is nothing to fear. We must be bold and strong in Christ to reach the very core of our heart. We must face what is there and with Christ overcome that deepest darkness within. When we have passed through this experience, we will look back and wonder why we were ever afraid!

Each day we must enter increasingly into the light. Each day we must bring one more thing out into the open to be exposed and overcome: for example, hardheartedness, meanness, pride, and haughtiness. As each one is brought into the light, we come closer to God. It may seem that the problems in our heart are endless, but we must continue regardless. Each day becomes a step closer to God. We continue day by day until we are fully illuminated, until our heart is filled with light, until Christ is shining within, the day dawns, and the morning star rises in our heart.[1] How unspeakable is that joy!

Relationships

Only let your manner of life be worthy of the gospel of Christ: that, whether I come and see you or be absent, I may hear of your state, that ye stand fast in one spirit, with one soul striving for the faith of the gospel ... (Phil. 1:27)

... make full my joy, that ye be of the same mind, having the same love, being of one accord, of one mind ... (Phil. 2:2)

In our relationships, whenever there is some issue between us and others, we must pray about that as well. We must search *within ourselves* for our own problem. What within us is causing the difficulty? When that is cured, the outward will follow.

We must not strive with others, but find Christ in every situation and for every problem. As much as possible, we must be at peace[2] with those around us. However, we must not compromise with the darkness, nor accede to the evil one. If we follow the Christ who is within us, we will find peace. Then, we must walk in that peace.

Together with our Christian brothers and sisters, we must seek one mind and one spirit. We must let go of our own opinions, our own ways, and our own preferences. As we practice this, bit by bit we will find ourselves thinking the same, being likeminded, and enjoying the same spirit.

---

[1] 2 Pet. 1:19

[2] Eph. 4:3

Arriving

Through such a practice, we will slowly be brought into oneness.[1] We will be perfected into one, and enjoy the oneness of the Triune God. Pride, self, opinion, contention, dissension, and rebellion will all be gone forever. We will view others as higher than ourselves. What a joy to have these evil things, which have plagued us for so long, gone and to so love our brothers and sisters as to hold them in the highest esteem. Upon our arrival there, in that perfected oneness, we will find that we have all things common. What is mine is yours, and what is yours is mine.

This is not our doing. This is not something that can be manufactured. We could never accomplish such a thing on our own. Rather, this is God's working within us, yet with our cooperation.[2] This comes about through Christ's indwelling: His living, growing, and maturing in us. It comes about by His perfecting work on the character of the believers. When we are brought to such a state, God is glorified and satisfied, the Lord's prayer is answered,[3] and the multi-faceted wisdom of God is made known.[4] It is then that the Lord will return to take those who are prepared and ready: *one in the field and one at the mill.*

---

[1] Eph. 4:13

[2] Phil. 2:12-13

[3] John 17:1-26

[4] Eph. 3:10

CHAPTER 8

The Wisdom of God

―――――――――

And I say unto you, Make to yourselves friends by means of the mammon of unrighteousness; that, when it shall fail, they may receive you into the eternal tabernacles. (Luke 16:9)

The Son of man shall send forth his angels, and they shall gather out of his kingdom all things that cause stumbling, and them that do iniquity ... (Matt. 13:41)

Let me ask a question that is seemingly unrelated to this book: will the people of Earth use money during the Millennium? The Bible makes it clear they will not. The Lord calls money the mammon of unrighteous. Money is unrighteous and evil at its very core. Furthermore, the Lord tells us that at the end of this age He will send forth His angels to remove everything that is offensive from His kingdom. This certainly will include any money that might remain, since it is unrighteous and offensive.

In addition, the Lord tells us money will fail. According to the context of the Lord's word, this failure will occur shortly before the millennial kingdom. None of us should think money or material wealth will last forever. On the contrary, at the end of this age, material wealth of every kind will fail.

So then, how will the people of Earth live during the Millennium? We must understand that there will be a great change at the end of this age and at the Lord's coming. Capitalism, socialism, communism, and any other kind of humanly devised government will come to an end. There will be no more money and no more material wealth.

You might rightly ask, *How will the nations subsist then?* The answer to that question has everything to do with what is revealed in Matthew 24:40–41.

Ruling

And the first came before him, saying, Lord, thy pound hath made ten pounds more. And he said unto him, Well done, thou good servant: because thou wast found faithful in a very little, have thou authority over ten cities. And the second came, saying, Thy pound, Lord, hath made five pounds. And he said unto him also, Be thou also over five cities. (Luke 19:16-19)

In the coming age, it is not only the Lord Jesus who will rule on Earth. Many of His brothers will reign with Him as well. To some, He will give rule over ten cities; to others, rule over five. He will share all that He has, including His authority. Now, consider this: if I cannot rule my own mind, how can I rule over ten cities? If I cannot rule my own emotions and my own temper, how can I rule over five cities, or even one city? If I cannot rule my own heart, I certainly cannot rule a city. To rule properly, my own being—my heart with my mind, emotions, and will—must be fully under my authority. Otherwise, how much damage would I do to those over whom I am ruling?

In this age, we are being trained to be the kings and priests we eventually will become. If we learn those lessons needed to rule and serve God in the next age, then we will enter into that age as kings and priests; if we have not learned those lessons, then we must learn them in the next age. This is what the parable[1] of the talents tells us.

To rule, we must be properly equipped. That is, we must be trained both within our own hearts and in interacting with others. If, in the next age, there is no money, no social construct to which those on Earth are accustomed, and no method of government with which they are familiar, how can they be ruled? In other words, what will those of us who are ruling over cities do to guide the people of Earth into that way of living with which God is pleased?

---

[1] Matt. 25:14-30

A Proper Living

How will the people of Earth live in the next age? That is, how will they behave? It will be nothing like what we see today. At this time, the whole Earth is encompassed by evil spirits, who greatly influence mankind and bring every human into the system of things on Earth, called the *world*. That world lies in the evil one.[1] It is ruled by Satan and all of his forces, who invisibly and deceptively control mankind. *That* world is incurably sick, and will be destroyed at the end of this age. God will end this evil world through the trumpets of His judgment.[2]

But how, then, will the people who remain on Earth subsist? How will they live? How will they maintain their existence? How will they provide food and shelter, since they know only their experience in this current world?

Since the world to which they are accustomed will no longer be, they must be trained in a new way. They must be shown how to live. They must be weaned from the evils and addictions of this current age, and learn a new way—God's way!

God's Way

What is God's way? It is to share freely of all that we have been given. The more we give, the more we are given. God is and has a boundless supply. There is no limit in any way to what He can provide. The great limitation to God is *us*, and what we are willing to give of what He gives us. The flow of supply from God is immeasurable, and we are the channels through whom that supply flows. If there are obstructions within us, then God's supply cannot flow. It will be the same in the next age.

The people of Earth must be trained to give freely. How will they live? By giving! How will they subsist? By sharing! As they learn to give, to share freely, to look out for the welfare of others,

---

[1] 1 John 5:19

[2] Rev. 8:6-9:21, 11:14-19

God's great and unlimited supply will provide them all they need. This will be a most wonderful existence.

What is this, in essence? *It is to have all things common.* Whatever belongs to one, also belongs to another. All things are shared and all things are freely given, without any expectation of recompense. This is how the people of Earth will be trained to live during the Millennium.

The Wisdom of God

It is not only reasonable, but should be expected, that what and how God is—in this case, having all things common—would be reflected in His creation. With such an understanding, it becomes clear why the evil one has led man into the creation of money and the many ways of obtaining material wealth and power.

In the Godhead, all things are common. As this age approaches its close, God will lead some believers into also having all things common. This, in turn, will be a prototype of the type of life God desires for those believers who are left behind to pass through the turmoils of the endtime. Finally, this way that the believers have learned will be passed on to all the people of Earth during the next age.

This way of being will become a template for all humanity in the new heaven and new Earth for the ages to come in eternity future. What God is doing in the believers today, or at least in those who are attuned to His heart, will be seen and experienced forever in God's new creation. How wise God is in His doings and dealings with man.

Eventually, the whole universe—the believers, Israel, humanity, and all the creatures—will reflect the selflessness of God's divine nature. Words cannot express the wondrous delight every being will then share. Can anyone imagine such wisdom, beauty, and glory!

CHAPTER 9

A Perfected Church

And the multitude of them that believed were of one heart and soul: and not one of them said that aught of the things which he possessed was his own; but they had all things common. And with great power gave the apostles their witness of the resurrection of the Lord Jesus: and great grace was upon them all. For neither was there among them any that lacked: for as many as were possessors of lands or houses sold them, and brought the prices of the things that were sold, and laid them at the apostles' feet: and distribution was made unto each, according as any one had need. (Acts 4:32-35)

    The situation in the early church shortly after the Lord's ascension was quite glorious. It was striking in almost every way, and very different from what we see today in Christianity. All the believers were one in heart and soul; they had all things common; great grace was upon them all; they lacked nothing; the word was spoken with power and boldness.[1]

    There were no offices as are so prevalent today. There were no deacons and, apparently, no elders. These offices simply did not exist. They were all brothers, as the Lord said we were to be.[2] There were only the believers with the apostles, who were praying and ministering God's word.[3]

    This was absolutely proper. The believers were taking care of each other: the older were caring for the younger, and all were giving of what they had and owned. It was a beautiful scene. What

---

[1] Acts 4:13, 29

[2] Matt. 23:8

[3] Acts 6:2

they experienced at that time was what was on God's heart from the beginning, and was how God Himself is.[1]

However, after a very short time, this experience in the church disappeared. Why did this happen? What was the real problem among the believers that caused this early church life to end?

Recovery

I know thy works (behold, I have set before thee a door opened, which none can shut), that thou hast a little power, and didst keep my word, and didst not deny my name ... (Rev. 3:8)

At the end of this age, the Lord will recover the experience of the early church. At least some of today's believers will practice what the early believers practiced. They will have all things common, as implied in Matthew.[2] Theirs will be a simple church, as depicted in the church in Philadelphia in Revelation. These believers will hold to three things: the Lord's name, the Lord's word, and the little strength they have been afforded.

The Lord's *name* speaks of His person. The Lord's *word* is the word of the Lord's patience. This is the hope of the salvation that God has promised to those who believe. Through all the trials of this current age, there are and will be some believers who keep the Lord's word steadfastly, believing in this word and into the Lord through it. The *little strength* is in apposition to the great power of the Spirit in the early church. Philadelphia does not display great power, but rather little strength. This little strength is the strength of the divine life within them.

In this way, the Lord will come full circle. He will bring about again what was at the beginning. Then He showed what should be: a prototype of the proper practice in the church. At the end, He will bring this back into existence again. However, there will be one enormous difference.

---

[1] John 17:

[2] Matt. 24:40-41

The Lack

Now in these days, when the number of the disciples was multiplying, there arose a murmuring of the Grecian Jews against the Hebrews, because their widows were neglected in the daily ministration. (Acts 6:1)

The wonderful scene depicted in the early church ceased because of problems. The first issue was seen in Ananias and Sapphira,[1] who withheld from the apostles a sum of money, which they had obtained from the sale of some property. They pretended to give all the proceeds from that sale to the apostles, but in fact, they lied. They lied not only to the apostles, but also to the Holy Spirit—to God. This cost them their lives.[2] However, it indicates that under the surface in the early church there were envy and self-glory.

Before the incident of Ananias and Sapphira, a brother, named Barnabas, had sold some land and given the money from that sale to the apostles, to be used as needed. Ananias and Sapphira, in an attempt to obtain the kind of recognition afforded Barnabas, pretended to do the same. But due to their greed, they kept for themselves a portion of the sales price. They were envious of Barnabas, sought glory among the saints, and displayed greed in their actions.

The next incident—one that effectively eliminated the practice of having all things common—was the neglect of the Grecian widows by the Hebrew believers. Some in the church, who were ministering food to the older saints, showed bias by neglecting those Jewish believers of Grecian origin. In response to this, the Grecian Jews began murmuring. Just like some in the wilderness murmured against Moses,[3] some of the believers in Jerusalem murmured. This showed the darkness and evil hidden in the hearts of those murmuring against brothers. This was a serious blow to the practice of the early church. Between the neglect of the

---

[1] Acts 5:1-10

[2] Acts 5:5, 10

[3] Num. 14:2, 16: 41

Grecian widows and the murmuring of the Grecians in response, this essentially ended the practice of having all things common, for it is never again mentioned in Scripture.

The next problem—one that was immense—was Judaism. Certain ones among the believers—the Judaizers—continued the practice of Judaism, especially circumcision and staying separated from the Gentiles. They practiced keeping the law, and by so doing were leading the believers away from God's new covenant. The old covenant in the Old Testament had come to an end.[1] God brought in a new covenant, with a new way. By leading the believers back to Judaism and the old covenant, the Judaizers were destroying the faith upon which the believers' salvation rested. In fact, the whole book of Hebrews addresses this serious issue within the church in Jerusalem.

Deacons and Elders

And the twelve called the multitude of the disciples unto them, and said, It is not fit that we should forsake the word of God, and serve tables. Look ye out therefore, brethren, from among you seven men of good report, full of the Spirit and of wisdom, whom we may appoint over this business. But we will continue stedfastly in prayer, and in the ministry of the word. (Acts 6:2-4)

To take proper care of the saints regarding practical matters, the office of the deacon was instituted by the apostles. Something had to be done to assure food was distributed among the believers in a proper and unbiased way. Apparently, the believers themselves were not generally capable of doing that. Rather than the apostles turning from their study and ministry of the word to wait on tables, certain ones from among the believers—ones who were full of the Spirit and wisdom—were appointed to attend to these practical matters. This was the institution of the office of the deacon. This position was established to solve practical problems among the believers.

---

[1] Heb. 8:7-13

The office of the elder does not appear in the divine record of the New Testament until much later, in Acts 11.[1] We are not told why it was instituted, nor is there a record of its beginning. It could be, and likely was, that this practice of appointing elders was borrowed from the Old Testament.[2] There, Moses was unable to handle all the disputes among the children of Israel. Therefore, he appointed certain ones of the Jews to be rulers and judges among the people. It seems likely the office of the elder came into being for a similar reason, to handle spiritual matters among the saints that could not be resolved by them. The elders were to oversee the spiritual welfare of the church. Properly, however, this should have been handled without instituting the office of the elder. It may have been necessary at that time, but as we shall see, it was not something that was according to God's heart for the Church.

God's Heart

And if thy brother sin against thee, go, show him his fault between thee and him alone: if he hear thee, thou hast gained thy brother. But if he hear thee not, take with thee one or two more, that at the mouth of two witnesses or three every word may be established. And if he refuse to hear them, tell it unto the church ... (Matt. 18:15-17)

But be not ye called Rabbi: for one is your teacher, and all ye are brethren. (Matt. 23:8)

In Matthew, the Lord speaks concerning problems between the saints. He tells us if one brother sins against another, the offended one should go to that brother and tell him his fault. If the sinning one does not hear, then the offended one should take two or three others with him to establish every word between the sinning and offended ones. If he still does not hear, then the offended one should take the matter to the church.

---

[1] Acts 11:30

[2] Ex. 18:13-26

The Lord's words are quite precise. He did not say to take it to *the elders* of the church, but to *the church*. If the Lord had wanted to establish an eldership within the church, He could have done so at that time with the insertion of three simple words. Had he inserted those words—*the elders of*—the eldership would have been established by divine authority. On the other hand, by leaving them out, He makes clear that according to God's heart there were to be no positions in the church.

Furthermore, the Lord tells us that we are all brothers, having one Teacher. None of us were to be above others. We all are on the same level. Some may be spiritually older, and others younger, but we are all on one level.

Indeed, in the last book of the Bible—Revelation—the elders[1] of the church are not mentioned. The epistles to the seven churches were not addressed to the elders of the churches, but rather to the messengers of the churches. This indicates the eldership is something temporary that will cease by the end of this age within the proper practice of the church.

The institution of offices in the church provided opportunity for all manner of evil to manifest itself: for example, the seeking of position, the desire for self-glory, and the institution of a hierarchy within the church. These are all absolutely against God's heart. None of the saints are to be above any of the others.

Furthermore, there is to be no one between the believers and God. Each of us is to have a direct relationship with Christ and God the Father. As we can see by looking at church history and the present condition of Christianity, the institution of offices within the church has introduced innumerable problems for both God and the believers.

It is true that bias, murmuring, greed, envy, and so many other dark things were among the believers in the early church. Furthermore, if we were to look closely at many of the believers today, we would find the same thing. So then, what was the actual

---

[1] The elders mentioned in Revelation are the angelic elders, who are before God's throne and overseeing the creation.

issue among the early believers, and how could it be different today?

God's Way

First, we must understand how God has been working in the believers since the Lord's ascension. He imparted Himself as the divine life into the human spirit of the believers.[1] This is called regeneration. Since regeneration, He has been working within the believers to spread Himself from their spirit into their soul. This is called sanctification[2] with transformation.[3] Eventually, He will spread from within the believers even to their bodies. This is called transfiguration.[4]

A young believer has the divine life within his spirit. But how about his soul? That soul is as yet little touched by God. Within the soul are many things of the believer's previous life, such as evil thoughts, desires, choices. As that person partakes of the divine life and allows it to spread from his spirit into his soul, the mind, emotion, and will of the person slowly changes. He is made holy, and transformed into Christ's image. This is the way God accomplishes what is on His heart. This way that God uses to work out His eternal purpose is called His *economy*.

Believers who are young in the divine life are prone to living according to their still-fallen soul, so that much of what they do expresses the evil that is in their flesh and then conveyed through their soul. There is only one solution to this condition, and it is not the modification of behavior. We may determine to give up being envious, but the envy will still arise within our heart.[5]

---

[1] John 3:6

[2] Rom. 6:19; 2 Thes. 2:13

[3] 2 Cor. 3:18

[4] Matt. 17:2; 1 John 3:2; Matt. 13:43

[5] Rom. 7:15

Our determination means essentially nothing. In fact, this becomes a frustration to God. The only solution is gaining God in Christ in our soul through the growth of the divine life within.

What was the real problem among the early believers? *It was their immaturity in the divine life.* They had little growth of that life. And along with that lack, they were to a large degree ignorant of the evil one's devices.

Unquestionably, the early church had much, but this was due to the Spirit being *upon* them.[1] Great grace was *upon* them.[2] So, as the Spirit's power and grace upon them slowly lessened, there was not yet the growth in the divine life within the believers to maintain the proper church practice. As a consequence, many problems arose, and this in turn necessitated the establishment of certain offices to help keep the church in a somewhat proper condition. This, however, was not God's deep desire. At the end of this age, the Lord will finally bring into being what *is* according to His heart.

Life, Not Power

As this age draws to a close, the Spirit is not as active outwardly as He was in the early church. By withdrawing Himself as outward power, He allows the divine life within the saints to grow and mature. As the saints can no longer lean upon that outward power, they of necessity must find and experience the divine life *within*, to uphold the proper living of the church according to God's heart's desire.

The Difference

What is that great difference between the early church and the church at the end of this age? In the early church, it was the Spirit *upon* the believers as *power* that produced the wonderful scene at the beginning of Acts. It was the Spirit upon the believers

---

[1] Acts 1:8

[2] Acts 4:33

that moved them to have all things common. It was the grace upon the believers that allowed them to live with each other without problems.

During the endtime, the church—or at least some believers in the church—will have an experience produced by the Spirit *within* them as *life*. It will not be the Spirit *upon* them moving them in a certain way, but the Spirit *within* them. There is an enormous difference in these two experiences of the Spirit.

As the Spirit slowly withdrew Himself as power to the believers in those early days, their true inward condition was exposed. That condition did not match the outward practice they had previously enjoyed. As a result, that practice ceased. This was what happened in the early church as seen in Acts.

At the end of this age the proper church life will come into being through the divine life *in* the believers. Since it is something springing forth from the divine life within, it is eternal. It is not produced by the Spirit upon the believers, for the Spirit can then withdraw. It is produced by the Spirit as life within the believers, and so can never leave and never change. Then, whether the Spirit is upon the believers or not will make no difference. The Spirit within the believers will produce their living.

A Comparison

And Jesus said, Father, forgive them; for they know not what they do. (Luke 23:34)

And he said unto him, Verily I say unto thee, To-day shalt thou be with me in Paradise. (Luke 23:43)

And Jesus, crying with a loud voice, said, Father, into thy hands I commend my spirit ... (Luke 23:46)

To better understand this difference, let us consider some examples in the Bible. The Spirit is not limited to the New Testament believers in His outward activity. There are numerous examples in the Old Testament of the Spirit of God coming upon men: Othniel,[1] Gideon,[2] Jephthah,[3] and Saul,[4] for example. But, did the Spirit upon these men change their heart in any way? Recall that Saul tried to slay David, even though the Spirit had come upon Saul previously. Perhaps the best example is Samson. When the Spirit came upon him, He was indeed mighty;[5] he was a kind of superman. However, look at his living. He was a womanizer and worse.[6] The Spirit upon Samson did nothing to his inward being.

On the other hand, look at the life of Jesus. Throughout His life the Spirit was upon Him working great deeds of power. Indeed, one of the first things the Lord uttered in His ministry was from Isaiah:[7] *The Spirit of the Lord is upon me, because he anointed me to preach good tidings to the poor: he hath sent me to proclaim release to the captives, and recovering of sight to the blind, to set at liberty them that are bruised, to proclaim the acceptable year of the Lord.* However, at the end of His life, as He was being crucified, and as God was judging Him for us and on our behalf, that Spirit of power withdrew from Him. That was a moment of great, horrifying darkness through which the Lord passed. But, this severe crucible made no difference in Christ's behavior. He still asked the Father to forgive the ones crucifying Him because of their ignorance; He still saved the repentant thief; He still entrusted His spirit to the Father.

It will be in like manner during the endtime. Some of the believers will experience the divine life to the full, mature in that divine life, and live it out. This will produce something both beautiful and *eternal*. It is this that God has desired from the beginning.

---

[1] Jdg. 3:9-10

[2] Jdg. 6:34

[3] Jdg. 11:29

[4] 1 Sam. 11:6

[5] Jdg. 14:5-6; 15:14-16

[6] Jdg. 16:1

[7] Is. 61:1-2, Luke 4:18-19

When this scene appears, it will bring the Lord back. He finds this irresistible. It will end the age, because there will be no more reason for God to allow this evil age to continue. In such a living, God will be reflected. This living is the divine Being lived out through the believers.

How sweet and precious this is. It is a prototype not only for all the believers, but also for all humanity. It is also a prototype for all creatures going forward unto eternity. Rather than fighting among humanity or the creatures, there will be sharing and goodwill. How sweet and precious this will be!

May we take these words to heart, and pray for God's desire. May all these words find a home in the hearts of those who are reading this book. May we all receive these words with seriousness, pray over them, and choose to live a watchful and prayerful life before the Lord. May this issue in a church practice in which Christ is manifested and in which God is deeply satisfied. And may we all, as many as are so minded, rejoice in the Lord's appearing from within us in that day.

A Perfected Church 87